Holy Karma

Holy Karma

Not a Religious Book

An in-depth look into Holiness

Sacred Secrets are Revealed

About your Natural Holy Self

Holy Karma

Dedicated to

the Holy Children of God

Loved Entirely and Eternally

Holy Karma

Dedicated to

Those in Holiness Arising

In Preparation for bringing
Heaven to Earth

Holy Karma

Your Holiness

Not the Body DNA

But your Holy Birth right

Holy Karma

SHAMARÉ

© Copyright 2023 Shamaré

Shamaré asserts his moral right to be identified as the author of this work.

All rights reserved. No part of this publication may be produced or transmitted in any form or by any means, electronic or mechanical, including photocopying, recording or information storage and retrieval systems, without permission in writing from the copyright holder.

Published by Heaven on Earth

www.shamare.com

shamare.guardian@gmail.com

ISBN 978-0-473-67076-4 (paperback)

ISBN 978-0-473-67077-1 (EPUB)

A catalogue record for this book is available from the National Library of New Zealand.

Contents

	Preface	xiii
	Introduction	1
1.	Holy Karma > Holiness is Birthed from a Single Point of Grand Holy Intelligence	7
2.	Holy Karma > Holiness in Expanded Holy Awareness	29
3.	Holy Karma > Holiness in Completion	55
4.	Holy Karma > Holiness in Knowing	73
5.	Holy Karma > The Holiness in Decision	93
6.	Holy Karma > Holiness Arising	125
7.	Holy Karma > Holiness in Self Love	137
8.	Holy Karma > Holiness in Clarity	155
9.	Holy Karma > Holiness in Joy	169
10.	Holy Karma > Holiness in Peace of Mind	173
11.	Holy Karma > Holiness in Communication	177
12.	Holy Karma > Holiness in Being	181

13.	Holy Karma > Holiness in Actions	189
14.	Holy Karma > Holiness in Serving	193
15.	Holy Karma > Holiness in Transparency	197
16.	Holy Karma > Holiness in Transformation	201
17.	Holy Karma > Holiness in Trans-Mutation	205
18.	Holy Karma > Holiness Lifts Great Burdens	213
19.	Holy Karma > Holiness Relaxes and Expands Awareness and Ability	221
20.	Holy Karma > Holiness in Heaven on Earth	227
21.	Holy Karma > Holiness in All Things	231
22.	Holy Karma > Holiness as Divine Wholeness	235
	Addendum 1 *Holiness Review*	243
	Addendum 2 *Holy Karma > Preparing your Holy Mind for the Holy Trek of no Distance, to a Place you have never left*	245

Addendum 3	249
Holy Karma > I release the need… A Universal Statement to Start the Healing of your Holy Mind!	
Addendum 4	253
Availability of the Information to your Holy Mind	
About the Author	257
Other Books by the Author	259

Preface

Holy Karma

*This book is not channelled from Jeshua Ben Joseph
like the last book but a direct writing
from the mind of my Holy Self.
However, the seed to start the book was a short,
channelled session from Jeshua
and is included.*

*The influence of Jeshua Ben Joseph
will be seen throughout the book,
as he has been the one entity
that has assisted mental changes for myself,
allowing the discovering of my own Holiness.*

There is always some reflection that takes place when your book is close to completion.

The big question, of course, is whether the primary reason for writing the book has been delivered in the words.

In this preface, I will offer a short summary sketch of what the book holds in the many pages, just to pique your curiosity and start the process of arriving at your own Holiness with Holy Karma flowing.

This book is an expansion of the first channelled Shamaré book *Spirituality 101–601 and Beyond*.

*This book's aim is to assist
as many incarnating souls on Earth as possible
to recovery and refind their own personal Holiness
and in the process of doing this start to live and walk
inside the energy of a new mental framework
called Holy Karma.
This is the state of complete mental well-being.*

You will decide whether the book meets its purpose of helping you to move to Holiness. This can take some time, of course, and it may require several reads. The book contains many new concepts that are discussed in detail.

This Holiness recovery state that leads to Holy Karma requires breaking free from the mental illusion and misperception of believing you are separated from God in some way.

*Holy Karma is the spiritual and conscious
mental operational state
that all incarnated souls will have to surrender into
to return to Holy Peace and Holy Joy
without this false perception of separation.*

Each person's Holy Awareness and Holy Self Love will eventually be elevated sufficiently that the final step to "Realised Holiness" will be just a natural last step. The book will lead you through information on this.

This "Realised Holiness" will allow each soul to fully

participate inside Holy Reality or Holy Home, once again running in the energy of Holy Karma which is Holy Cause and Holy Effect.

This book will be of value to the many now wandering down the various spiritual roads leading them to this "Realised Holiness" with Holy Karma flowing inside their lives.

You might be amazed at what you read in this book and how close you are to your own Holiness moment by moment.

You are closer to Holiness than the width of a thought.
Does that seem possible right now?
Read on; you will see it is possible always
Just some encouragement.

This book uses the word Holy continually throughout the text. This book is quite unique in this respect.

This is very deliberate, as the word "Holy" acts as a major textual meaning differentiator between two possible opposing mental states.

Holy in this book carries the meaning of "Whole or Complete in a Divine Way".

This is the state all will return to after the dream of separation from Holy Source God is ended.

Holiness,

*therefore precludes "The mind of ego self",
the misperception of "self as human body",
which is a complete denial of
Holiness.*

This is a key point in the book and is discussed in many ways.

You are not the created DNA Human Body!

This book also uses capital letters often to delineate between Holy Reality Information and lower case for misidentified non-holy ego misperceptions.

Additionally, you will find some text that is centred and in italics to highlight some ideas or concepts, like the sections above and below. These become standouts if you are just flipping through the book.

*The meaning and outcome of Holy Karma for you,
in your ongoing incarnated life, will be unique.
The ego world viewpoint will have great difficulty
in understanding the Holy Karma meaning
that you personally discover,
as the world's ego intellect is never able
to fully understand Holiness.*

The ego world as a whole is blinded to Holiness with ego misperceptions, ego misidentifications and will continue to live in complex dualities, with the base emotional and mental states of fear, guilt and judgement, until the discovery, for each, of their own Holiness at some point.

It will happen. It does happen.

This book is recommended reading for all those desiring to recover their own Holiness and then to allow and surrender to the Holy Karma flow of Divine Cause and Effect that runs the Universe.

This is not a study book.

You do not study to enter Holy Karma,
or have to believe something to achieve Holiness,
or even believe Holy Karma
exists to arrive at your Holiness.
Holy Karma will appear naturally
when Holiness arises.

Holiness is your natural mental and emotional birth right.

You chose to return to Holiness by using your great power and desire to heal your mind and then finally surrender to your own Holiness and live inside Holy Karma energy.

This will arise for you easily,
if you get out of the ego way
in Holy Mental Surrender.

These points being offered in summary are big clues about the book for you all > Enjoy.

All the best to you all, as you delve into this information, as it prompts you to live inside Holy Karma with your own personal Holiness once again.

Some of you may find some of the words
and concepts confronting,
just push through
but
recognise the emotional effect as curious.

Ask: how and why is this so confronting to me?

You might as well start the process right here at the Preface.

Jeshua just prompted me to say to you all, "Waste not another moment"!

Love to you all from Shamaré

The Protector
The Door Keeper
The Gatekeeper
The Guardian of the Holy Karma Arising Now

Introduction

Holy Karma

How did the two words "Holy Karma" come together for this book?

It is extremely rare to find these two words "Holy" and "Karma" together, side by side!

Most would see karma as a negative concept or bad energy. How can it be Holy?

In fact, in the last Shamaré book, *Spirituality 101–601 and Beyond* that discusses many features of spirituality in depth, the words "Holy Karma" appear only once, in Chapter 601.

Let's examine the surrounding paragraphs (below) of Chapter 601, to gain an understanding about "Holy Karma". It may take some time to come to a full realisation, many ups and downs along the way.

But of course, in Reality, we are multi-dimensional entities, and a major piece of us remained safely intact in oneness and right-mindedness always. This right-mindedness is a composite of the Holy ALL. The Divine Itself, and is therefore shared among All, as it originates from the Only One Thing that truly exists at all moments, God Itself.

It is a Pure Spirit Composite of All Spirits, undefiled and Holy, and hence called Holy Spirit, or Divine Spirit. A Dimension of True Self that is always available. This Holy One (The All) lives in Holy or Divine Spirituality, or Whole Spirituality or Natural Spirituality or Original Birthed Spirituality or in "Holy Karma".

The adding in of "Holy Karma" happened only in the last edit on the *Spirituality 101–601 and Beyond* book, just before going to press, and for very good reasons. Jeshua and some of the ascended masters wanted it added and the two words are a pure summary of those many other words and concepts in those paragraphs.

Hence the two words become a very useful metaphor and therefore can be used as an excellent teaching tool symbol, revealing a set of Holy Revelations and Holy Concepts.

The two words also appeared, of course, so I could write another book and expand on this concept of Holy Karma. I know Jeshua will be very pleased with this discussion on Holiness and Holy Karma.

As you read on, the concept idea and term, "Holy Karma", leads to a very broad edifying Holy discussion and it is to be viewed as personal info for you the reader. No comparisons with others!

Wrap your Holy Mind in these Holy Concepts as the book unfolds.

> *You are reading this in your Holy Mind right now, you will see this has to be true as you read on.*

It is food for your Holy Mind and Holy Heart.

> *"This book could really be endless as Holy Karma is the Holy Universe Itself in Action, endlessly unfolding, in Holy Divine Operation with Infinite patterns of activity from infinite souls in Divine Purpose, with the Holy Cause driving Holy Effect (You)".*
>
> *Holy Karma = Holy Cause and Holy Effect*

Another point to note about this book, *Holy Karma*, is that it is of a different nature to the book *Spirituality 101–601 and Beyond*, as it can be read differently.

Spirituality 101–601 and Beyond required a linear read from front to back, as the themes and core concepts add to one another incrementally, to help lift the reader to a greater understanding of spirituality and leading to the point of "surrendering misidentified ego".

This book, *Holy Karma*, after reading the Introduction and Chapters 1, 2, 3, 4, can be read in random order.

It is even possible to flip through all of the book and find highlighted centred italics text that will assist in your mind healing. These are little highlighted snippets to ponder.

The book's purpose and design, therefore, is to elicit remembrance, emotion and imagination from deep down, at the Wonder of Divine Holy Self and Divine Holy Universe and then allowing Holy Karma to bubble up once again and reign supreme in your life, as one of the "Holy Begotten Children of God".

We all have earthly families in this created realm that we love being around to share life's experiences with (mostly!) This book introduces you back to your "Original Holy Family" whom you have spent eternity with already.

You will find Chapters 1, 2, 3, 4 quite deep. Other chapters are short and very concise and obvious.

As you read on further, there may arise up for you a strong awakening desire to "stay the course" and continue in a progressive way, to arrive at "Full awareness in wonder, living inside Holy Karmic energy".

"Reawakening of course and living in Holy Karmic Energy is to become the Holy Instrument that projects and creates Holy Effects driven directly from Holy Divine Cause".

Surrender into your Natural Birthed Mental Holy State of Holy Karma as soon as possible.

Use this book regularly to top up your Holiness gas tank; even one page or a single paragraph can shift your emotional field and bring peace to your mind, by recalling your mind back to the Holy Karma flow.

*Because of those two words "Holy Karma",
I have been given this opportunity, once again,
to write another book to engage your Holy Mind
and your Holy Emotions.*

*To assist you to finally throw off the limits
of ego DNA body-centric humanity
and ego misidentification
and let your Holy Mind explode
into the vastness of Holy Karma once again.*

And in this process, to live life in an entirely different way, without fear, guilt and judgement, in Holy singularity once again, which is sitting continually in Divine Love Flowing, in great joy and peace of mind, participating fully in Holy creativity of the new project arising of a new Heavens and a new Earth.

*It only requires a simple desire to change
and grow the "Love for Your True Holy Self*

and then make a Personal Holy Decision".
The Holy Decision can only be made in your Holy Mind.

Enjoy the expansion of your Holy Mind, with wonder, and ask how all of this can be so true for me.

Love to you all from Shamaré

The Protector
The Door Keeper
The Gatekeeper
The Guardian of the Holy Karma Arising Now

1.
Holy Karma > Holiness is Birthed from a Single Point of Grand Holy Intelligence

Hello to all my Holy friends once again,

Yes, you are Holy! Don't believe it? Well, read on.

> You are actually "Incarnating" into a place somewhere inside the Divine Mind, called earth.

> Yes "earth and more" sits inside the Holy Mind as a creation. The so-called Matrix!

Incarnating means mentally projecting into the experience of "living as flesh" or "knowing flesh".

Consider the words above: you are not the DNA flesh!

> You are instead projecting your mind and then you have the experience of knowing the experience as flesh.

> Who is the "You" that is doing the mental projecting?

> What is the true nature of the "You",

that enables it to project its mind, to incarnate into flesh for experience?

Two little points to stop on for a few moments to contemplate.

As you sit quietly now, allow yourself to become that "You" for a moment or two.

Feel that, know that. You are participating in this right now without effort. It is that easy.

That is the Holy You, projecting for experience, looking at this page. Feel that looking.

To get things started, I thought it might be helpful to give some background information on how the book initially began. It started with this short channelling below once again from Jeshua.

This arrived in my mind one afternoon, as the "Starter" for the new book. I was sitting again, and it came up in the mind to type it up.

It was typed without plan or thought, just an allowing of the channelling to flow out through Holy Self.

It may be helpful to read and consider them, since we are going to be discussing how to surrender into Holy Karma or Holiness in the Spiritual Domain, with some great detail, in this book.

There is much to say. Lots of pages. You will not be the same after the big read.

A little more base Holy Info about this 3D space and time domain will be helpful in cracking open what Holy Karma is really about.

The start of the book was early 2020, sitting quietly one day in March, it arose inside the flow of Holy Karma and was typed up.

So here is the channelling from Jeshua and my Holy Self, as I received it.

Actually, he was just talking to me in the Real Mind, of no distance.

"Consciousness arises from a Single Point of Grand Holy Intelligence."All Consciousness is tapped and tied to this Single Holy Point and therefore has this original Divine Holy Source as their life and love feed.

Inside this Consciousness, there also arises "Awareness of a Holy Self" or "Spirit Individuation as a Soul".

These Holy Selves or Individuations all naturally discover a playground where all can come together, communicate together, to create together, called the One Mind, given as a free Holy

Gift at Holy Birth to all the Holy Children: you included.

This One Mind is infinite, open and complete in Holiness.

Streaming forth from this "Source of Consciousness" is the life-sustaining and emotional energy, best described as "Divine Love Flowing" (Holy Love Flowing).

Tied to this energy is a default mental and emotional state for All in the Divine Love Flow, of great joy and endless peace of mind.

This is the grand birthed inheritance for All and of All.

This is the Divine Family's mental state as the Holy Begotten Children of God, made in the image of the Holy Source.

This Holy Peace arises from the "Singularity of Love", as there are no other contracting energies or thoughts.

This is Heaven itself; this is Holy Love itself and all are connected directly and immediately with all others inside this Holy Source, without differentiation or specialness.

All are equal, with free will to create and act as they will, inside the Holy Karmic arrangement.

The Singularity of "Only Love is Real" resides inside this Domain called our Reality or our Home.

Harmony surrounds All, with no Dis-ease or dis-function. All is allowed, All is trusted, All is embraced as wondrous and pure.

Purpose is not thought of and is not in debate but entirely obvious; that is, creating more of the same, in a myriad of forms, with delight. A veritable paradise of purpose with creation and the generation of more.

Therefore, it can be said that "Expanded Consciousness was a spontaneous spawning of the Holy Source and has always been, as no sense of beginning exists".

Time is not here.

That was it, the transmission covering Consciousness, Awareness and Holy Karma.

And with that truly revealing
and wondrous opening statement,
we as the Holy Children,
move into the second book on Holiness
and Spirituality, titled Holy Karma.

Holy Karma, the grand gift for all the Holy Children to reside in, to use and play with.

And if this is your dream to be in this play area of Holy Divinity, this book on Holy Karma will lead and encourage you to keep moving, changing, shedding ego connection and projection and expanding back to your Holy Self. If you are just curious, continue on, as much will be said and revealed.

Consciousness, Awareness and Holy Knowledge is ever expanding and what has been unknown in this ego world domain for many eons is now starting to be revealed and expanded. Many of you will know and feel this expansion already, naturally.

Some of these Holy Concepts need to be discussed, understood and expanded. (These concepts are actually ancient information and now is an important time to reveal them once again.)

To start looking at these revealed Holy Concepts, let's look at a common question asked by so many incarnating as humans over the many ages they have resided in this 3D space and time domain.

The big question!

"Why the physical universe, earth, human bodies and the world experience – with so many difficulties and

unknowns?"

There are many other questions like this, but this is one of the simple base core questions asked so often and begging for an answer to assist in the release of new concepts, to allow the expansion of the restricted ego consciousness and awareness that humanity seems to live inside of.

Scattered around that base question, there are many auxiliary questions, also asked for eons:

*Does God love us?
Are we abandoned here?
Will good win over evil?
Where can I find peace of mind?
Am I really sinful?
Will I go to hell?
How do I live in Joy inside this Domain?
How do I overcome the struggle
and mentally heal myself?
Where are the answers?
Are there answers?
Will humanity sort things out?
What do I need to believe?
Do I need to believe?
Am I truly loved?
Do I need a saviour?
Is there a saviour?
Am I really Holy?
Does Holiness really exist?
And many more; the list is endless.*

The ego intellectual minds have made myriad attempts to answer these types of questions.

Many books, thoughts and ideas have passed through the world domain. Even so-called Holy books.

Some are even angry about these types of questioning. They say there are no answers.

Some have become resigned to not knowing any answers and they somehow accept their lot in life.

A Holy answer to this one base question would be very useful and would lift the veil on the unknowing.

The lifting of this "unknowing veil" will become a lightbulb moment for many readers.

Much will start changing in the mind of those that have these Holy Knowing and Holy Concepts.

Holy Awareness increases naturally
with the realisations of these Holy Concepts.
It is not learning anything new; it is becoming aware
and the holding of your evolved expanded viewpoint.

A Holy viewpoint.
You will and can actively evolve yourself
after knowing this information.

So, back to our question,

Why the physical universe, earth, human body and the world experience with so many difficulties?

To arrive at the Holy Answer, some additional Holy information will be added that will allow the Holy answer to be assimilated easily.

Some understanding of the Holy activity of Holy consciousness from ancient times is required to appreciate this Holy answer with understanding and knowing, for our time period.

So, let's get into the Ancient consciousness process that occurred long ago before the physical universe, earth and incarnating human DNA bodies.

In an ancient time in the Holy Family's only dwelling place naturally called Reality, at some point, a thought arose in the Holy Mind of souls living in the simplicity of singularity, where "**Only Love is Real**". This thought arose in the Holy Mind/s that dwell in Reality (Holy Home), and not anywhere else.

The question that arose in that innocence was, of course.

What would it be like to live in a place where "Only Love is Not Real or True"?

That is a very big innocent thought or question. Right out of left field maybe!

It is impossible to experience the answer to this question in Reality because only Holy singularity is flowing in Reality, with a base energy of **"Only Love is Real"**.

So the developing process that occurred from that innocent question was the beginnings of creating for ways to experience the thought of living inside a domain with **"Only Love is Not Real"**.

That is, dwell in a different mental domain than Home Reality, with the possibilities of developing mental dualities, like love and the opposite energy, and from that simple start point develop many more dualities, a myriad in fact, with great complexities.

This innocent question/thought would necessarily lead to the need to step out of Reality Holy Home where **"Only Love is Real"**, so as to experience these types of dualities.

However, literally stepping out of Holy Home is not possible at any time, you can't leave Reality Holy Home ever. Therefore, another mechanism had to be developed to make it possible to experience the dualities of the original question or thought.

So, right at that very moment of **"that Innocent Question"**, creative action started to allow for the experience of it somehow.

This creativity started right inside Holy Reality, right inside the Holy Mind.

In fact, "Only in Reality", as there is nowhere else to create and experience anything.

Consider that last statement carefully also: there is a strong message in there for you.

Over time, many differing creation types arose to allow many experiences of these dualities' concepts.

The earth, the world and humanity are just one of the many and a very good one to get lost inside of.

And you know that this is a true quality duality experience from seemingly living in the earth, the world and humanity experience. Love is not the only energy present in this experiential domain and the opposite energies and duality actions are truly possible to experience and understand.

With time, more and more dualities or polar opposite energies and actions evolved. This evolution led to great societal and mental complexity. No longer would there be harmony and simplicity, like there is in Holy Reality's singularity, with **"Only Love Flowing"**.

> And yes, here we are
> seemingly living inside the effects
> of that ancient question.
> That innocent question started a process
> to allow the creation of this system for us,
> with more dualities created in front of
> our human faces day to day.
>
> You experience them regularly;
> you actually create them often yourself.

Another question arises from this creativity. How did we actually leave Holy Home then and go to a new domain to experience all of this?

As already stated, to leave Holy Home is impossible and therefore this experience of dualities, earth, the world and humanity is only had by mentally projecting into a virtual domain; that is, a creation.

This world creation is virtual reality at its best.

> Note that point, that the experience is had
> by mentally projecting
> from Holy Home into the experience
> and not actually living in the virtual created domain.
> It is a developed expanded mental ability
> that makes it possible to experience dualities.

Something else to understand that goes with this

incarnated virtual experience is very important for your mental health right now.

Yes, we did actually ask to be part of this virtual experience, that is why we seem to be here! It is not by accident. You are one of the brave ones or the crazy ones that put their hand up and said pick me, me!

Now let's keep expanding this duality projection concept.

*Get this concept embedded
deeply in your understanding.*

*"It is not possible to experience a duality creation
in any other way, other than Virtually."*

*"In fact, it is not possible to experience any creation
other than in mental projected virtuality."*

*"This is the demarcation
between Reality and any creation."*

*The preface of Jeshua's A Course in Miracles
written in the 1960s
gave a very strong hint about all of this.*

What is Real cannot be threatened.

What is unreal doesn't exist.

*Herein lies the peace of God.
Real = Holy Home*

unreal = creations requiring mental projections.

Let that sink in a little!

In that ancient time of the arising innocent question, we definitely knew that we could not bring that concept of dualities into Reality Home.

So mental projection as a tool was developed and honed to allow mental perception inside a virtuality or a creation.

And so, what are you experiencing as part of the group that said "I will go virtually (by mental projection) and seemingly live mentally and emotionally inside these dualities and experience all that goes with it"?

You may like to smile about that agreement.

Yes, you did actually put your hand up and say, "Include me please."

The person with the clipboard told you to go down to door number 23 and wait until you were called.

Was this a mistake by you or was it something far more?!

No mistake. A lot of discussion beforehand, of course.

"Do you really want to go, Jimmy? I have packed some sandwiches for your lunch, just in case you get hungry!"

It was to be another grand mental virtual projected adventure.

And just in case you haven't digested this fully yet.

3D space with time, the physical universe, is one of the many creations that arose from the ancient innocent question. Yes, the physical universe is a creation and floats in the One Mind of Divinity.

Ask yourself, where else could we put it? That is the right thought right there, nowhere else, of course.

This virtuality is a place to play in, a virtuality room, a non-reality and hence it only exists as long as we need it.

So, it is not permanent, nor will it exist as it is now, long term.

We can translate it to something else, if we like. *That is just a teaser piece of info.*

It hangs together in created time until the creators of the experience say enough, we are done now.

And there you have it, the answer to the perplexing

big question that all of humanity have asked at some point.

> *"Why the physical universe,*
> *earth, human body and the world experience –*
> *with so many difficulties."*

A virtual play thing was made by us, to experience duality, with mental and emotional effects, long ago.

How is it for you in this created experience? Hmmm.

"This innocent question and the answer concepts" will be themes throughout the book.

Now, in Holy Reality where we exist always and only, the energy is **"Only Love is Real"**.

No dualities in reality; this is our Holy Home. A single energy environment.

This is the Divine or the Holy dwelling place for consciousness and awareness.

It is not a mental projection, or a creation held together with a thought or an idea.

It is the "Original and the only true energy of the Spiritual Real Universe".

Holy Home is rock solid, unchanged, unchanging and unchangeable.

We are residing in that right now, never leaving, even if you think you are living on an earth somewhere!

There is nowhere else to go to that is real or permanent.

> **There is only Holy Spiritual Universe**
> **or our Holy Home**
> **where consciousness and awareness exist.**
>
> *All other experiences are virtual in nature*
> *and only happen by mental projection*
> *from inside the gaming rooms of Holy Reality.*

Reiterating, a non-reality experience, like this 3D universe with an earth, space with time, can only ever be experienced inside Holy Reality by mental projection, as a virtuality.

This is what you are involved in day to day, moment to moment, right now reading. Hmmm.

> *You are reading this in Holy Home right now.*
> *Now that is a very big trick.*
> *Be slow about moving past this line.*
> *Consider it carefully and well.*

From Holy Home, that is our reality, we can remotely look into this very small physical universe, of earth, human bodies and the world experience and seemingly project ourselves in to it and virtually live (incarnate), taking up residence in a DNA body (embodiment), a biological robot that we can control with our minds remotely from Holy Home. Like a Wi-Fi link. Ha.

This mental projected connection is extremely accurate, high speed, high resolution, with DNA cellular linkage and light tight.

And why? To make the perceived experience you have asked for seem very, very, very real.

The realness of this virtual state is called immersive and is essential for the duality experience to seem so true. Just like the virtual reality headsets that humans play with now.

What would be the point of having only a partial experience of dualities?

Have you explored its virtual boundaries yet?

The biological DNA body robots are an awesome design
with an extremely powerful central brain processor
that runs the projected programs
in parallel like a super computer,
with superb hi-res cameras,
high-fidelity microphones
and loud speakers,
they are mobile, and biologically self-healing

and you can also make new ones by physical birth.

A dream design for all human mechanical robot designers and builders, even now playing inside the virtual game.

When we are all complete with this virtual game, it will pass away as a translation when our mental supporting projections are redefined and the energy holding it in place causes transmutation.

This will happen when Holiness has the last say because the original innocent question has been fully experienced and answered.

We will decide it is over when we have gleaned all we need from the experience of dualities.

Much like when you decide to release an old mental or emotional wound and the effect drops away and you are mentally healed and translated to the new you.

It is over and done with and you arise as a new improved model. Ascension!

So how does that sit with you? That is the main part of the Holy answer!

It is quite a big mouthful to chew on but not so indigestible; maybe for some!

The concepts are simple, we already know about virtuality, as in this virtual domain, we play inside another virtuality all the time with screens, and it is OK. This virtual action in human incarnation is double virtuality! Seems OK! We manage well. It is not a hurdle or a difficult concept.

We turn the devices off, put them down and walk away, no problem, while sitting in Holy Reality.

To help engage your Holy Mind to settle down to the answers to the big why questions (why the earth, etc?) just a little further, you may appreciate the next chapter's new expanded explanation and discussion.

It is important to get these concepts
thoroughly embedded in the mind
because without these your consciousness
and awareness will not be operating correctly
or effectively and you will believe you are limited
to being stuck inside the virtual experience,
thinking it is reality
and you are just Jim or Mary,
a human DNA body.
Just an intelligent animal, as some say,
in the ego world!

Love to all those with imaginations safe enough to envision all of this.

Love to you all from Shamaré

The Protector
The Door Keeper
The Gatekeeper
The Guardian of the Holy Karma Arising Now

2.
Holy Karma > Holiness in Expanded Holy Awareness

To help expand on the last chapter's virtuality concepts, let's try to reverse engineer the first "Original Big Question" using what we seem to know already, even as incarnated ego-based humans that are endeavouring to expand awareness.

> *"Why the physical universe, earth, human body and the world experience – with so many difficulties?"*

What do we seem to know already, even at an ego intellect level?

We do know we have consciousness and awareness; that is, that we exist and act as an entity.

So how did we get here: to earth?

We seem to be on earth, so we must have got here somehow (maybe incarnation is an idea) into a third-dimension domain with dualities, with some awareness.

That word "incarnate" is very old and often is used to define the possible process.

A little more knowing with expansion!

In this earth domain, true divine **Peace, Joy and Love** are present.

The three energies are fleetingly present, only present some of the time.

Love is there when you smile lovingly at another.

Also, when you reach out to help, it is there in those moments.

Joy arises from having family.

Peace of mind is found sometimes in work, art, music, meditation or a holiday etc.

However, dualities generally rule this domain.

Further and because of the dualities, we also do know, the opposite polarity energies are present much of the time and are around every corner. Even to hatred, wars and genocide of biological bodies.

*These knowings do lead a mind that is
growing in awareness to work out
and understand that something different,
something new must have been made or created*

> *outside of Reality (Holy Home),*
> *to make it possible to experience*
> *the Energy of "Not Love".*

This ego system, running with "not love" as a main energy, is the main reason for all the human questions!

If you are suffering, you often wonder about love, peace and joy: where are they to be found!

So, this is a good start with our ego intellectual growing awareness knowing. This is only natural thinking based on feelings that arise with the difficulties.

Additionally, the design of this created domain certainly allows for or provides the opportunity to experience the effects of seemingly living a life outside Holy Reality, in many complex dualities.

So, we do know the creation is a good design model and fit for purpose. It allows for the experience.

More dissection for knowing:

This next part is very logical.

> *The creation, therefore, is a very clever design*
> *and a purposeful creation*
> *and would provide answers to the question:*

> **"What would it be like to live in a domain**

where only Holy Divine Love is not Real?"

This original question from long ago has to be answered thoroughly and we are the eager participants in this process. Door 23 and the waiting room. Door 22 and you would be somewhere else!

That is why 3D space and time exist, so we can answer this question by experiencing dualities of many sorts, with the use of a remote virtual link from Reality Home right into the created earth domain of experience.

To be able to have a place of experience in virtuality, matter also had to be designed and made. This required development by adding the new ability to use the base energy available in Reality Home of light to be transmuted into matter. This new developed ability was a very Big Bang moment when finally, light was translated into matter.

All sort of new possibilities arose to make the experience in virtuality more interesting. Most do not know this information yet!

If we wanted to experience separation from Holy Family, why not make a world with separation already built in? Bodies create beliefs in separation and cause fear to arise due to vulnerability.

You are over there and I am here,

> *I am vulnerable to you.*
> *Hence the dualities of separation and danger*
> *drive the ego system*
> *into creating safety systems,*
> *make groupings or nations, borders and countries,*
> *police for inside, armies for outside,*
> *weapons and much more.*
>
> *We do understand these sorts of ideas and functions.*

These next few concepts we know and understand very well in life as an incarnated human.

All of this linking up in virtuality is like remote linking to computers and devices these days.

Sit in another place on the planet and drive a device somewhere, without actually being there.

Sometimes you don't even know where the device is, but it can be controlled and driven.

That is why we can say, we seem to be connected up and live somewhere on a place called earth.

Virtuality from a Holy family's home of Reality by remote linkage is not a big conceptual jump!

How are you doing?

> *Where is Earth really?*
> *It sits in the Divine Mind where all ideas sit.*
> *It cannot be anywhere else.*

And who really cares? We are linking up and playing, having fun remotely and experiencing all of it in the Holy Reality's Gaming Room. Thank heavens for door 23.

> *"What would it be like to live outside Holy Divine Love Flowing?"*
>
> *My God, really? Yes, you do know.*
>
> *Pass another sandwich that your mum made for the trip, Jimmy.*

Also consider this.

Why not get to experience all the duality types thoroughly while we are seemingly here?

Experience it fully, in all the shades and levels.

Let's not mess around: experience our projected creation fully, touch the boundaries.

And we also do know now: we can actually do this and we are doing it well.

Consider all the ego cause and effects running that we generate in the Holy Mind but act out in a body.

And now you can see that this is an amazing step into imagination or a creation of virtuality.

It is purposefully building creation mechanisms to

allow the trialling of that original innocent eons-old question.

> *"What would it be like to live where*
> *Holy Divine Love Flowing*
> *is not the only energy flowing*
>
> *but opposite energies are possible also?"*

There are many more questions, of course. You ask them often.

Was this project meant to be permanent?

Were we meant to get mentally stuck inside this mental projection or incarnation, in virtuality?

Were we meant to go completely insane and believe we are the biological body inside the virtuality, that we march around with while we are seemingly present?

"Imagine this scenario: one day a technician in NASA, Houston, goes to work and starts thinking they are the remote-controlled Rover on Mars that they are controlling millions of miles away."

Now that would be insane. I now identify as the Mars Rover.

That's how it is for all humanity at present, thinking they are ego human body stuck here.

Oh yes, have I said ego misidentification is totally insane. Ha.

We know this can be true for us also, as we have been insane or maybe still are, especially about this concept of being a DNA body.

Another conclusion or ego knowing that does arise from our continuing expanding awareness in our virtual earth experience.

"This virtuality, 3D domain with time, has to be outside of any Holy Divine Reality."

Just by intellectual deduction, none of the goings on in this domain could ever happen inside a Holy Divine Reality. Not possible back home in Holy Reality; the police would come! Ha.

Also, more intellectual deduction with appreciation now!

Since this incarnate experience does not seem to be inside Holy Reality, it must be a very clever contrivance of some sort, a mimic, a toy, a creation, a model, a gadget, a virtuality, a guise, a play thing, a new hobby room, a mental projection, something to play in and with, to experience dualities while sitting inside the thoughts of separation from both the Holy Family and the True Energy of "**Only Love is Real**".

*Those thoughts of separation from God
and Holy Family or the Holy Divine Body itself
and this finally leads to thoughts of separation
from your Holy Self*

*Hence depression and self-loathing
are common among the players
who are insane and think they are
Jimmy, Mary or the Rover!*

Quite the Mental Contrivance, like fifth-dimension chess. Have you mastered the game?

Is there an end point? What is the end point?

Something additional to ponder on, again arising from ego intellectual knowing, which is distinct from Holy Knowing.

A Holy Self inside Holy Reality could not reside and live with such an idea or concept of believing in Holy Divine separation. You can agree with that, without believing in Holiness.

So, to allow the experience of that unholy thought of separation concept, a "mimic you" arises to allow the experience of this thought. And of course, living in insanity, believing instead they are the robot not the creator. This is called misperception, you are misperceiving who you really are.

And so, it becomes true for the all the incarnating souls. You know this from experience also.

An isolated ego self
(an alternative you, named Jim or Mary or Rover)
arises for the experience,
and that is how it is for all in the game.
I am the Rover, believe me. I can prove it, you know.

Listen to me, I am not crazy.
Pinch me and see if I feel it.

It does seem that All in the game
have had to become a "misidentified self",
to experience this virtual arrangement,
actually holding insane thoughts
of having Identification
as a Biological DNA Body
and not True Holy Spirit Self.

That is the depth of the game and the madness inside it. Love it!

Try to tell someone you are not Jim or Mary but a Holy Child of God; you will get some funny looks.

However, it is all still an innocent experience! No one can get hurt. However, mental suffering can and does occur. It need not be though, as we will see soon.

What are the results of living as this ego misidentified biological body self?

Because of incarnation and bodies,
fear, guilt and judgements appeared,
and these were the first base sets of dualities.
Next we then learnt the art of mentally projecting
out into this human world
Divine Holy Love in many distorted forms,
transmutated forms,
often as the opposite
of Holy Divine Love, in many shades,
so it all can become true in and as insane dualities.

We are all that powerful
and it was all just to experience
the multitude of dualities
that would arise in a world where
"Only Love is Not Real".

Was that helpful? That may be very useful. Have a chuckle.

Not a big stretch for you really, as half is very obvious, even if you do not have Holy Knowing yet.

What an amazing creation we made to experience this, with so much detail and contrivance.

Incredible biological self-healing DNA bodies, with body birthing, with multitudes of natural knowing earth systems to keep our incarnated adopted bodies alive and well with amazing food, oxygen, water and much more.

That natural is there as an "earth creation knowing system" (the mother ship, as the sustainer and provider) that acts as true virtual nature or the natural in this unnatural alien domain.

Some worship this "nature" in error. It is only a creation, not the designer creator.

*What an amazing experience
and yet it is often clouded entirely
by the difficulties of living as "a small ego self",
in limited consciousness and awareness,
with dualities and the losing touch
with our Holy Singularity True Spirit Self.*

So enough on these base ego questions of "Why" that arose inside the experience.

The whys are often just victim thoughts. Not too helpful, unless you need to wallow in it all.

Let's now look at another set of interests that has absorbed human ego minds for millennia.

*This "Time Period" in the earth, world,
human experience,
is of great interest to many.
Are we approaching a change of some sort?
Can you feel it brewing?
Is there about to be a humanity collapse of some sort?*

Humanity is riddled with thoughts and writings of apocalyptic endings. Are these going to come true?

Well, that is why you are here right now. You have come to witness and participate in a change. You want to be part of it.

Many entities are also looking in through other windows in other Domains, at what is progressing here.

The future is not known, nor can it be predicted. Where humanity goes is not defined. No Predestination.

Trends can be observed and guesses can be made of outcomes. Divinity or Holiness will always prevail against misidentified ego insane ideas. That is a given. Holiness beats ego creation every time.

At this point in human history,
the experience of living in dualities
is getting more difficult and complex.
Humanity is finding they are running out of ego ideas
or suitable ego solutions to keep the experience of
earth world humanity stabilised and running.

The experience or experiment
is staggering to an end point
where ego misidentification must be relinquished
to complete the whole project in success.
That is awakening to Holy Self inside

the ego dream of Divine Holy separation.

Does this mean we will experience an apocalyptic end?

No, instead a miracle will progressively occur with many awakening to rediscover True Holy Self once again, with expanded Holy Consciousness, Holy Awareness and Holy Knowing, and awakening inside the virtuality creation experience. The awakening experience is in the Divine Mind only, of course, in the room where all the insane ego minds seem to exist. Ha.

This has never been done before that we know about and will be setting a precedent for All Consciousness. This is called the "Grand Awakening".

Awakening from the dream of the dreamer
that believes they are a Human body
and are separated from their Holy family
and live on a planet called Earth somewhere.

Having tried almost all possible combinations
of duality fixes and solutions
inside beliefs, cultures, power groupings, philosophies,
governments, wars, intellectualism, laws,
politics and religion etc.

It is time for all those thinking they are stuck in

the ego body experience to look in other new Holy directions for a better answer.

And here you are, having come to this point, here right now, with you sitting reading these words.

Well timed and on cue. At last, you say!

How is it for you, after reading all of this?

Amazing, well done.

You have been pondering about all of this for a while now!

What was it that brought you to this moment?

Yes, we understand this, we have ALL been there also.

It is the private moments that are the powerful ones. When you sit with your thoughts and emotions in quiet times. Allow these emotions to flow as they carry the message for you.

Do listen carefully for the small voice of reason,

> Saying, "My Holy Child it is time to awaken now, you have done well, but now it is time to come home."

We are almost full circle in the earth, world, human dualities innocent experiment.

We have tried almost every mental ego contrivance to make things right inside the duality of virtuality but with no real lasting success.

There is a song inside those words I feel.

We have rediscovered, from this experience, that truly
"Only Love is Real"
and works!

The ego algorithm must be faulty? Ha.

The ego computer is overheating and malfunctioning or the ego code is faulty or the ego data is full of corruption or all of the above. And we have ego power problems to boot.

Metaphorically speaking!

Complexity upon complexity arises, with more distortion and insanity and solutions seem sometimes to be further away than ever, often just about to be captured but sliding away, unavailable.

Touch an ego sacred idea and everything shudders. Introduce a new belief and many resist it.

*And of course, it had to be this way,
as how can a system (dream) based on beliefs
in separation from Holy Divine Source,
misidentification of self, living as in a false ego mind,*

> ever be Peaceful and full of Joy,
> with Holy Divine Love Flowing.
>
> **Impossible!**

It is, however, what we asked for and planned for. What a great tangle that has developed.

An experiment that went awry.

> However, "**Only Love is Real**"
> and we all must choose now
> and return home.
>
> Many Ascended Masters have said they do not want
> to be assigned to this recovery project,
> it has become too crazy.
>
> Actually, the recovery is ours now,
> we are the Masters now,
> and the purpose inside this virtuality is to finally act out
> of Holy Karma flowing once again, in singularity.
>
> Holy Karma,
> Divine Cause driving Divine Effect at last,
> still in innocence.
>
> Surrender of ego is coming for many.

As we have seen and experienced, it is not a Holy natural thing to try to live in this duality domain, unless something rather miraculous like Holy Karma arises to restore Love.

And now, be very pleased with yourself that what is arising in you (and the many now) is this new energy that is searching and asking for a better solution, a better outcome, asking for an Arising Mind Miracle.

This newfound curiosity, sitting in a strong desire, will continue to bubble and grow until the arriving Holy Miracle turns into Holy Karma itself.

> *Thy will be done on Earth*
> *as it is in Heaven,*
>
> *prayed trillions of times,*
> *is coming true at last.*

Into the earth, world, human's immediate future experience, a great longing will arise from many egos, based on this agreed-upon simple thought.

> *"There must be a better way to live",*
> *we have tried almost everything else as little ego selves!*

Yes, the asking for a Holy Miracle to arise somehow!

Maybe a new creation of some sort to start!

Maybe expanded consciousness and awareness. We sure seem to need it now!

Yes, an arising new agreed Holy Co-creation is coming.

An adjunct Holy concept will be added into the original innocent question.

A mechanism of recovery, rediscovered.

> *Actually, the Ascension Recovery Mechanism*
> *has been there from the beginning*
> *for anyone to avail themselves of,*
> *placed there by a loving head of the Holy Family,*
> *available to all.*
>
> *A bridge back home.*

A new algorithm is to be inserted into the duality mental experience by our choice.

And the algorithm is Holy Karma Arising, yes? And we will put it in place; yes, we do this by choosing.

The Holy Karma Miracle is:

> *Awakening and knowing fully even inside*
> *the ego duality experience that, in fact, you are*

> **"A True Holy Self".**
> **Holiness itself.**

Is this possible?

You are doing it right now, just sitting there imagining such a thing!

> *Imagine more each day until you are transformed*
> *and only sit in Holy Karma.*

*"The new Arising Holy Desire is to heal mental distortion
and return to True Holy Home
and become True Holy Self."*

Additionally

*To be "Nurtured once again inside
the grand Spiritual Uni-verse
of the One Divine Turning,
our place of Singularity,
where **"Only Love is Real",***

**your now remembered ancient birthplace
of Peace, Love and Joy with Holy Family.**

Yes, you are now once again re-remembering your True Holy Family Home Life and longing for its return. You can actually say to yourself, I am reading and knowing this in the Holy One Mind right now!

The earth, world, human experience is all only metaphorical and virtual anyway, to play with and you have done this well in this incarnated theatre of creations, in the madness, thinking you weren't who you really are.

And you are the generations to bring the Miracle, Holy Karma into Action, inside the Virtuality experiment.

*"The Meek", the "Holy Miracle Seekers",
become the "Holy Miracle Makers",
that will inherit the earth after all.*

Please step into stabilising your mental and emotional search and journey right now, knowing this one fact as true and pivotal, and hold it close to your life's experience from now on.

> *"That All Creations
> are Unreal"
> and are made
> as mental projection
> from Reality Holy Home.*
>
> *Just for experience.*

And where do you think you are incarnating right now?

Yes, right answer.

> *This is a Non-Reality,
> it is Unreal, because it is a creation
> and only continues to exist by mental projection
> from Holy Minds inside Holy Home*
>
> *and, therefore, it does not really exist permanently
> like Holy Home, Holy Reality, Our Holy Rock.*

A little more on this.

> *The "True Holy You" dwells perpetually in
> the Spirit Domain,
> never leaving and you are only experiencing incarnation
> by projecting mentally inside this*
>
> **earth, world, human experience,**

which is just a creation.

Once you have this concept locked tightly, you are away on the Grand Awakening journey safely and permanently and will become one of the "Holy Miracle Makers" that journey inside Holy Home.

Allowing Holy Karma into this earth, world, human experience creation is an amazing concept. Think and imagine about that coming.

As always, mental
and emotional Holy Progress
is only a simple decision away,
to release ego-fixed attention
and move freed attention to
the new Holiness Arising.

So let go of the old un-real or created stuff, that is the chains of the burden of ego DNA body misidentification, thinking you are the DNA body named Jim or Mary. Already dropped the Rover idea!

Holy Expanded Consciousness is just around the corner.

After digesting any of Chapters 1 and 2, you may need a mental and emotional rest.

Did I hear you say, too right, this is amazing stuff? I am exhausted!

I am sure you will read these chapters several times.
Please do, it is sometimes required,
as the ego's stubbornness is well known.

Only if you have eyes that can see,
eyes that can penetrate through
the fog of ego misidentification,
will a new arising Holy Vision arise for you
from the flow of Holy Self Love.

You may even find yourself having a deep DNA body sleep to turn off the thoughts and concepts.

Welcome back after the tenth read. Yes, it was quite heavy going.

Read it again after your mental rest until it is not heavy any more but becomes light and simple, allowing Love, Joy and Peace of Mind to flow once again.

When it is light and simple, the new concepts are bedded in, with no need for any more discussion or dissection.

The new Holy Natural Arises, the Miracle,
as expanded consciousness,
and it was just a simple change of mind.

I Am a Holy Child after all, amazing!
I thought I was Jim or Mary. Ha.

Or the Mars Rover, just for a little while anyway!

Also notice, it does not require a new belief to make it true, just knowing and feeling it and allowing it.

Also, no faith is required, as you are now aware you are always inside Holy Reality itself.

No hope is required as what can you hope for when Holy Karma arises in your Holy Mind once again.

Yes, a return
to your natural Holy Mental state once again,
inside the Holy Home we were birthed into.

Not that you ever left; it was just an illusion of mind.
Hence the journey home is
a journey of no distance, to a place you never left.

It has also become very obvious now.

You are much more than the
"Body Experience of DNA Flesh
you think you have been having".

That new knowing will amaze you
and liberate you and set you even freer.

You will be amazed more yet; you will even weep a little or become very emotional; allow this!

And so, I will leave this chapter at this point, to allow for mental rest, some cogitation and reflection and another sleep. Then on to Chapter 3, "Holiness in

Completion", which will add a whole new deeper layer for you. Can we get deeper? Yes, but simpler!

Love to all the Seekers and Deciders

Love to you all from Shamaré

The Protector
The Door Keeper
The Gatekeeper
The Guardian of the Holy Karma Arising Now

3.
Holy Karma > Holiness in Completion

You have no doubt picked up this book to access some suitable spiritual food, something to feed the inner craving of Spirituality and Holiness you are becoming aware of, that needs feeding.

The food is in the form of clever symbols for eyes that may evoke memories, imaginations, emotions and thoughts, to assist in your Transformation and Transmutation of Mind, back to "Holiness in Completion", to live again inside the framework of Holy Karma flowing.

> And just to set the stage and tone
> for the rest of the book for you mentally,
> you are already "Holiness in Completion",
> only dreaming otherwise!

> Say to yourself, "I am Holiness in Completion",
> just to try it on.

What was the emotional kick back? Sit in the emotion of doubt or confusion until it dissolves.

You may be living in a dark mental ego shadow

that seems to make knowing your *Holiness in Completion* distant or clouded and mentally far away from you.

*However, if Holy Possibilities
have not shown themselves to you yet,
they are waiting in the wings,
never lost, just dormant,
like a hibernating bear.*

Your Holiness can never be lost, as you will see!

Your Holiness is actually your natural Holy Mental state but at present may be the "Forgotten or Hidden Mental State".

This Chapter 3 is a further expansion of Chapters 1 and 2, to develop more fully these Holy Concepts.

Yes, this is possible, even though Chapters 1 and 2 were quite a jump. We are going to jump more.

Let's get straight into it.

We will start at this very historical point, yes, at the beginning of all things, "that is Consciousness being a Singular Point where all things spin from, and this does include you".

First point, notice Consciousness is not written as Holy Consciousness. The reason is that

Consciousness can only ever come from a source of Holiness or Completeness or Divine Wholeness.

*"Consciousness Arises
from a Single Point of Grand Holy Intelligence."*

Try saying this to yourself now!

"I arise from a Single Point of Grand Holy Intelligence."

Yes, and how does that feel? Did you doubt?

Notice the emotional response kick! Sit in these feelings for a few minutes.

Where does your Consciousness, Awareness and your Life all arise from?

It is a gift to you, your treasure, because the result of it all is the amazing you.

You may use the single line of words above, as a mental recovery tool, a way to reset to a peaceful mind, and in the process of recovery release the misidentified ego mind tricks of diversion that will arise day to day, moment by moment.

And there are many! You have practised them all very well, even honed them to precision.

Just say this to yourself, as a mental reset tool when any and all mental distortions start taking place.

Say to yourself:

*"But wait, I just remembered,
I arise from a single point of Consciousness
with Grand Holy Intelligence."*

The distortions and madness will most probably slide away, especially if you can laugh about it all. Make it fun; you will laugh at first because it seems untrue, but later you will really laugh because you know it is true.

And if the madness doesn't dissolve, those mental distortions effects need to be sat in for a while until you can allow Love to flow again and let the distortion dissolve away.

And you might well laugh when you realise it is not serious at all. You are safe always. Loved always.

Eventually you will laugh a lot more as things get less and less serious in nature and then one day Joy pops up and then Peace of Mind invades your Holy Mind once again.

Holy Karma starts flowing again. "Holiness in Completion" raises its head. It was like the bear hibernating. Springtime had to come to the cave and now it needs feeding! Wild carrot greens first.

Continuing on in our first line.

*Also now notice
the first line does not say "All Consciousness"
but just "Consciousness",
as there is "Only ever One Source
of Consciousness (God),
because there are not several points (Gods)
that have ever created other consciousnesses".*

*God is a word, a term, a concept idea only.
Accept this.*

I am not talking about an old man with a beard sitting on a throne somewhere!

*All souls have this gift of consciousness and are tapped
and connected to this single point,
locked inseparably forever
and therefore have the
"Original Source of Consciousness
as their Life and Love Feed".*

You cannot lose this connection ever! We would all cease to exist if it was lost. The gift flows endlessly to all, to sustain all things. Love flowing.

In fact, this connection to this single point is so thorough that the "Blending or Emulsification of this Consciousness makes it indistinguishable between Original Source Point (God) and You".

This is true for the ALL, for all the Holy Children,

made in the Holy Image of that Consciousness, always and forever.

Consider and say this!

> "The Father and I are One!"
>
> "The Mother and I are One!"
>
> "God and I are One!"
>
> "Source Consciousness and I are One!"
>
> Nothing else exists!
>
> Everything else is a creation.

It may feel strange; however, it is the ancient remembered relationship arising.

These are mere concepts words again. Eventually you will not need concepts, as it will all be natural and normal again with no explanation required.

What is … is!

Consciousness Reality is unchanging, unchangeable and unchanged, even after all this supposed time.

> You can't alter who you are.
> You can only pretend to be as an ego self.
>
> As the ego is only a construct and a projection, not the True YOU.

No beliefs or concepts are required to awaken and change, your personal experience is the only proof and reassurance required. This is called Holy Knowing. This will arise for you. Not intellectual knowing.

Feel this and know this Holy Relationship.

Continuing on:

> *Also, inside this "Consciousness of Infinity"*
> *there is always*
> *"Awareness of a Self or Spirit Individuation,*
> *as a Child of Source, a Holy Child of God,*
> *Loved always, nurtured and always loved."*

Also, all the Child Individuations discovered long ago that there is a natural playground in this Consciousness Reality (multi-dimensional domain) where all can communicate and create.

A miraculous open unedited arena of mental play.

With full mental freedom. Holy social media! No edits, no deletes, no cancelling, no fact checkers.

> *Many in the virtual humanity experience*
> *are now realising and know*
> *that this is the required default mental status for*
> *"all experience to be authentic and worthy".*

Mental freedom is your gift forever, even unto madness inside ego mind, with no interference.

Mental Freedom is given as a gift to all, the family inheritance and this system is called the One Mind.

> This One Mind is also known as
> "The Christ Mind", the mind designed
> and set aside by Divine Source
> for the Birthed "made in the image of,
> the Begotten Anointed Ones or
> All the Holy Children of God
> to play in.

Just sit and consider how miraculous this One Holy Mind is!

You use this mental gift all day long. You never think it won't work. Sometimes it may seem a little tired or noisy or cluttered!

It is where everything takes place, all Perception and Experience.

> "This One Mind, The Christ Mind, is Open, Infinite and Complete in Holiness."
>
> No loose ends.

This is not religious information. This is base Holy Life information; you need to remember and move into it.

So, let's consider some of these words above for a moment.

> Why all the Holy, God, Christ, Divine, Spirit, Begotten words etc?
> It is because we need words to use as Concept Differentiators.

These Divine Words are used to separate Divine Concepts from ego world's concepts.

These Divine Words are used to separate Reality Perceptions from ego world's misperceptions.

These words are used to differentiate between these two mental states.

Reality Holy Ego and created human ego. Divine Ego and small misidentified ego.

True Spirit Self as Spirit and incarnated misperceived human DNA body self and other concepts.

> The True Spirit Divine Self is magnificence, God like, part of Divinity, Holy always.

> The ego body mind self
> is a small compromised misperceived concept, using a form of distorted mental projection.

> It doesn't really exist permanently as we all know, body death ends it.

How can you explain these two states any other way without those Holy words?

All languages and cultures have these types of special words to allow the differentiation.

Language is built around Holiness; it is encoded this way in DNA and not by accident.

These words are needed for our Holy Discussion and the Holy Transformation of humanity.

Heaven on earth awaits.
All societies can imagine this heaven state because of previous knowledge.

You have experienced this before and always remember the Love, Joy and Peace.

Have you noticed now that most human protests directed at world ego governments always include the remembered words "Love, Joy and Peace" as major themes?

Was that helpful?

You can now see this is an expansion on the Chapters 1 and 2 concepts and you thought you had absorbed enough already. This is going way out, so hang on to your hat.

To make it possible for you,
just let the Divine words

*flow over your mind
and allow transformation of the ego mind
that may be resisting such ideas.
Imagine all of this strongly.
Imagination is one of the best transformational tools.
It fuels re-remembrance.*

You can't imagine what you do not know!

Many are angry at God or their True Self, for seemingly abandoning them to ego mind. However, it was our choice, we did not have to lose Holiness in the experience. However, consider how crazy it has all become now because of the forgetting. The full Monty!

This anger will pass. Holiness will arise in completion, if desired and allowed.

Just get over it. Remember the waiting room at Door 23 and the clipboard person. You said yes, yes. That trapdoor was a little scary though.

Continuing on in expansion:

*And so, a Domain of Holiness, the only True Reality,
with the One Mind,
is where you dwell for Eternity in Awareness.
Yes, "Your True Reality, your Dwelling Place,
always and forever".*

You are there right now! Just asleep at the wheel

dreaming, or maybe sitting in the gaming room with a remote game control.

You are dwelling in Holiness itself, but just running an illusional concept in your mind, in slumber or dreaming separation from Divine Source. Let it go!

There is no leaving Reality ever!

You can deny this, but it doesn't change it at all.

*Even when dwelling in complete ego denial,
you have the original birthed gifts
of consciousness and awareness
and Holy Love flowing endlessly.
You are still alive and aware!*

*Just in illusional dreamed madness for experience.
Original Question again!*

Continuing:

Streaming forth from the Divine Source of All Things, the Single Point of Consciousness, is the Life and Love giving, outstanding, sustaining and emoting energy, best described as "Divine Love Flowing" and it flows through all levels of Reality's many domains, sustaining, motivating and supporting, and that flow always does include you right now, even when dreaming madness inside a virtuality.

Never separating nor dividing, nor creating specialness, with "All Equally in the Flow of Divine Love".

> The result of this Divine Love Flowing is a default "Inherited Mental and Emotional State for All, as the Begotten Children of God, and that State is of great Joy and endless Peace of Mind", beyond ego human comprehension.
>
> The Family Inheritance for all, as an endless gift.

Begotten means not created as new but replicated, or cloned, made in the Holy image of that one Source.

Same Holy attributes, same Holy substance, same Holy energy signature.

Yes, this is you in True Reality as Spirit.

Your grand inheritance with Holy Love flowing freely at all moments.

No dis-ease, no arising dis-harmony, is here.

Yes, this is you, in True Reality. Accept this for yourself and be transformed.

Say
"I choose this Holy Mental State for myself now!
I choose to see all things through the Christ's eyes now!"

*The result = Holy Karma arising,
Holiness in Completion arising.*

It will come as you allow more and more mental and emotional change with a final Surrender.

Dwelling knowingly again with your True Family as a Holy Child of God, always and forever.

This Divine Peace arises from the Singularity of Divine Love, with no corruption, no contracting energies or thoughts and it flows to and through you, bathing you endlessly in Holy affirming family connection and devotion.

Yes, this is you in True Reality.

*In complete security, safety
with "Holiness in Completion",*

Living inside Holy Karma.

It cannot be any other way. If you sink down to the source of all things, you will find yourself there sitting and waiting quietly.

This is Heaven itself; this is Divine Love itself and all are connected directly and immediately with all others and to the Root Divine Holy Source, without differentiation or specialness, with No Gaps.

All Holiness together.

Yes, this is you in True Reality.

Weep over these words and thoughts. You may allow those feelings to flow out and then you can get wrapped up in the arms of Holy Family once again. You were not forgotten or abandoned, and this day had to come for you when you would choose again, to re-join consciously to your Real Holy Family, dropping the dream of separation.

All are Equal, with free will to create and think as they will it, sitting inside the framework of the Flow of Divine Holy Karma.

> *"Holy Karma flowing out as the*
> *Divine Will, as Divine Purpose,*
> *as Divine Cause or Holy Motivator,*
> *moving to produce Divine Holy Effect,*
> *resulting in Divine Holy Action,*
> *and manifesting as Divine Holy Outcomes".*

Yes, this is you in True Reality awakened.

Harmony surrounds All and All is allowed, All is trusted, All is embraced as wondrous and pure and Holy.

Yes, this is also you in True Holy Reality. Awaken now! Trust the invisible promptings.

Purpose is not thought of here in Reality and is not in debate but entirely obvious and creating more of the same, in a myriad of forms, with delight, ceaselessly.

> "Spurting forth more Divine examples
> of many shapes and shades".
> "A Veritable Paradise of Holy Purpose
>
> and creation and the generation of more."

Yes, this is also you in True Holy Reality.

In Holiness in Completion, bringing heaven to earth as guided by Holy Spirit.

Therefore, it can be said.

> "Consciousness was a spontaneous spawning
> of the Divine Source
> and has always been, as No Sense of Beginning Exists."
> Time is not here!

And with these grand expansive set of statements in Chapters 1, 2, 3 never said to humanity before, in so much detail, we continue to move quickly and more deeply into a second Shamaré book on "Holy Karma", the grand family gift for all to use and play inside of.

Divine Prompting and Divine Direction:

> "Holy Karma, the Divine Cause and Effect,
> that will operate in all Holy Minds,
> awakening from the sleep

and the dream of Divine Separation.

"Holiness in Knowing" will now be looked at in the next chapter.

Love to all moving towards the Holiness in Completion.

Love to you all from Shamaré

The Protector
The Door Keeper
The Gatekeeper
The Guardian of the Holy Karma Arising Now

4.
Holy Karma > Holiness in Knowing

Now as we move deeper into the main body of the book, consider this.

Why are you reading these words? Is it that you desire true knowing, not concepts?

There will be "many current mental prompting mind events" that arise in an incarnated human ego mind, they will show up regularly now, and manifest at some mental and emotional level for the all.

Thoughts of "There must be a better way to live!" My God, where is this world going?

You are not alone in these thoughts, as almost all minds are jumping into these thoughts now.

Maybe just as feelings, or dreams, or events day to day or thoughts that won't go away, reactivity being observed, a malaise, an unsettled disposition, a desire for change, a remembrance of old, a loss of faith in the ego system.

These prompts are arising due to the Holy Spirit in Action. This happens whenever you allow an emotional and mental opening. Holy Spirit flows through all minds and around all consciousness and is with you always, lovingly assisting and helping to open your mind to emote, question and search and to rekindle the desire to awaken from the dream of the dreamer and "Know Again", with a reconnection with Holy Home.

Holy Spirit saying and planning,
"Maybe I can talk inside this dreamer's dream a little,
I have seen them stir a little during sleep.
Maybe this is a good opportunity to drop a few thoughts in the mind.

Awaken and remember Holy Child,
you are not forgotten or lost".

You are Loved always.

You may have neglected these prompts for many years, being too busy or occupied by many human family responsibilities, distracted or thinking you can solve it all yourself or that humans will as an ego group.

At this point in the book, the question, like this one below, may have arisen in your mind.

"OK, so how can all that above wondrous information about my true Holy family

> *be true for me and yet here am I, right now*
> *seemingly in 3rd dimensional space and time,*
> *on a planet somewhere called Earth,*
> *ensconced in a body with limits,*
> *using jelly eyeball to examine*
> *these symbols of communication??"*

Yes, that is a good natural ego victim question, and the ego does not know the answer. The ego Intellect is unable to answer thoroughly these thoughts that arise, leaving an empty feeling, an abandoned feeling, a resentment feeling, a disappointment feeling.

Hence all the searching and questions! I want to Know!

Yes, this body-centric incarnation state does seem a huge step away, both mentally and emotionally, from Reality Holy Family with Holiness in Knowing.

This ego not knowing is due to misperception and misidentification of self. The great ego blinkers.

So, to move past this unknowing state, say this regularly to yourself:

> *"I am misperceiving my life and myself.*
> *I now chose to awaken and remember*
>
> *and "know" who I really Am."*

In ego mind body life in the world, there does seem to be this big gap between "Playing in the One Holy Mind, fully connected with All and in great joy" with "Holiness in Knowing" and the "Incarnation into Human Body with dualities and complexities and great so-called human difficulties and suffering".

To round out this thought for you.

To your surprise, know and recognise this one point also: your ego experience right now is all taking place inside the Holy One Mind and not in an evolved animal DNA body brain inside the Third-Dimension space and time continuum. Many will have you believe this is how it works. However, your mental experiences and consciousness and awareness only ever exist in Reality Holy Home's one mind, always and forever.

Now to add another deeper layer in the discussion.

*Therefore, you are always playing
your incarnated mental game
inside the One Mind in Reality
and not in a body DNA brain.*

Get that sorted.

*This information is of great interest to all.
You are actually Home already, and your experience
is in Reality Home always.*

Say this to others and see what they say.
They may get it also.

To reiterate this thought slightly differently.

You are powerful to be able to do this
trick of mental deception.
Even though you are in Reality Home always,
somehow, you've tricked yourself into believing
that your experience is not taking place in the Holy Mind
but is all happening in an evolutionary-built animal
DNA ego body biological brain mind.
Impossible of course.
There is only the one Holy Mind to experience anything.

Some ego-based scientists will try to convince you
that it is in the Brain,
but they are unaware as of yet!
Some do know! They just don't know where the mind is!

By now the questions must be arising: "How do I untangle myself from this ego misperception and get all the Holy Knowing answers?"

The best place to start is right here, right now. Know this clearly, your so-called Human life pathways and experiences plus all the decisions and all the people in your life, all have led you to being here right now, with a distorted mental framework that needs to be undone and allow "Holy Knowing".

So, start the untangling right here and work back

into so-called incarnated lifetime experiences where there is so much misperception development and a myriad of beliefs.

The life pattern for all is almost the same: developed misperceptions leading to more and more belief structures with age, with more dualities and limits always. Civilisation it is called! It is 180 degrees out of phase with Holy Knowing.

> *Uncivilization is the ego's end point product,*
> *it would seem!*

So how does the untangling work?

You can now use this arising desired Mental Holy Energy state to start healing all your created ego misperceptions.

> *All those "How and Why" questions arising*
> *in your ego mind*
> *can now be used by you as levers to*
> *awakening yourself spiritually.*

> *To Holy Know again.*

Use these many mental recognitions, and new awareness, thoughts and feelings as the start point to awaken to your True Holy Identity, with True Holy Perception and Holy Knowing.

This does mean it is possible to transform and heal.

Over this life as an Incarnated Human, you may have read and studied some of the world's ego philosophers, even followed an egoistic religion, joined in ego politics, maybe even received an ego education but even still asked these life questions many times. The How's, Why's and What's.

Inside those ego-world modalities and institutions of learning, you may have found some release but many of those "How's, Why's and What's" questions keep persisting.

The reason for the persistent thoughts is probably because there are no real good fundamental ego answers coming forth to answer these life questions, often more ego cult thinking, with more conflicting beliefs and dualities.

Remember the original innocent Question that started it all?

"What would it be like to live in a world where **"Only Love is not Real"**?

Well, here you are experiencing it all as desired and assigned.

Doing well, suffering quite a bit. Suffering need not be. Chose again. Choose Holy Knowing.

Suffering is part of the experience of joining any of the ego belief cults.

It didn't have to be like this though, it just ran away on everyone into total insanity. Ha. What an experience – all self-inflicted.

A little Truth for you at this point to help the awakening and progressing Holy Knowing.

Once you realise that your personal misperceptions and beliefs that you have developed for yourself are the only and best place to start the healing of your mind, the quicker will be the unravelling.

Hold this fundamental realisation tightly and then away you go on the discovery to release all those ego misperception and ego viewpoints. All those dearly held beliefs and idea attachments, the reactivities.

This Holy Realisation is an act of Self Love, a Holy Moment, a Holy Knowing = Emotional Knowing.

> "I desire to heal myself, now!"

You are basically saying now as you progress:

> "I, as Holy Self, will decide how it is now,
> not someone else, not some other ego cult
> or another ego idea or a new ego belief.

I release the need to be or feel as a victim."

This simple mental shift from victim to searcher will start the natural flow out of victimhood to curiosity, and new power will arise in you to hunt out the answers and release yourself from the ego bondages, into Holy Knowing once again. It is only a few mental steps away.

This is Holy Power arising, flowing inside the framework of Holy Karma leading to Holy Knowing.

You are moving into Holiness again. You cannot fail. Ask and you will receive!

Celebrate this.

And why not start the journey with some big questions first!

Take up the challenge.

Little questions are ... only little.

You will discover also that all the big questions are also ... only little.

Awakening souls who have made this mental shift and appreciate the arising opportunities, who are examining their conundrums in earnest or better in delight, will never stop allowing more understanding on these seemingly perplexing opposites.

Question everything! What is driving me to get upset. Look beyond reactivity and find original cause.

Be driven by thoughts like these.

> "I have decided, I will search out
> the answers for all these questions for Holy Self.
>
> I release the need to feel stuck."
> Be gentle with self and others.

Over time, aha moments keep happening and healing of your Holy Mind will continue in earnest.

This method of simple questioning yourself leads to more and more mental transformation.

> Leading to the final point of mental surrender
> to the "Original Divine Will of singularity again,
> with Holy Love Flowing unmodified and uncontracted,
> now living inside the flow of Holy Karma".

> This is Holy Knowing

That is the recovery from ego insanity to Holy Sanity and end of the game for you and the experience can be written up and stored. You are now living inside Holy Reality, as experience.

You will reach this Holy Mental decision point where you can say this also:

"Not my will be done, but thine"!

Now you understand that historical Garden of Gethsemane moment. It is also your moment each day, moment by moment. Step into it, do not deny it. Catch yourself sliding.

Some additional info on this Gethsemane moment, in case you are interested.

This was one of the last healing moments Jeshua Ben Joseph allowed to flow through his Holy Mind before his Incarnated Body Death. You can see he was even having ego doubts on body death.

This was his Full Holy Mental All Surrender.

Even on the Cross he was still allowing healing of himself.

"Forgive them for they do not know what they do." No projection, remaining Holy (Peaceful and Joyful).

Release of all judgement. Moving into deeper and deeper Holy Knowing.

And you have crucified yourself many times.

Sometimes you may sweat blood on this stuff, or it feels like it.

Let it happen, do not back away. Courage will lead the way. It will be a transformative moment.

Others will want you to be kind to yourself but ignore them, step into the arising Holy Opportunity always, in courage.

They are sleeping, you are awakening.

A little more on Jeshua Ben Joseph.

He says even after 2000 years he is still evolving and growing in Holiness.

> This does indicate
> that "Evolving Divine Consciousness"
> is a continuing process forever.

> You are included.

Holy Divinity and Consciousness is expanding, and you are participating.

Now a definition or descriptor if you want one on Holy Karma.

> "Holy Karma flows out as the Divine Holy Will,
> from Divine Cause, to bring about Divine Effect,
> by Divine Action, and resulting in Divine Outcome,
> all happening while in the mental states of

Holy Joy, Peace of Mind and Love Flowing"

With Holy Knowing. In Holy Karma singularity.

Hence the Book's title: *Holy Karma.*

This is where we are going with all the words.

This book is for you to reach that point of mental surrender into the Holiness in Knowing, inside that framework of Holy Karma.

In doing so, you become Holy Effect once again, not ego effect.

In other words, you are back Home in Holy Reality, inside Holy Singularity, no longer projecting ego self.

You will have dropped misperception of self, have allowed Holy Self to re-appear or re-awaken. It will happen.

So, in summary, this is the funny or peculiar game everyone in incarnation is playing right now.

*Thinking they are awakening
inside the Third Dimension Virtuality,
just to discover they are actually always dwelling
in Holy Reality of Holy Home,
and you are just awakening from a chosen
dream ego state of experience right in there.*

You can laugh at that, but that is how it is.

Amazing, you say.

It is like a sudden switch in perception.
From one type of knowing to another type of Knowing.

From ego knowing to Holy Knowing.

You will not be the same after becoming aware of this Holy Knowing.

And if you are still just on the edge of this Holy Knowing, or you are very new to it all, it is OK, as what is started in your mind cannot be stopped now. You have called out.

You are on a pathway to mental change, with new Holy Viewpoints. You will start to see things differently now.

The Arising Holy Energy that is driving the spiritual search, for some, may fundamentally be linked to this deep personal emotion you have.

"I can feel deep down a great longing
to return home to my True Loving Holy Family,
to be nurtured inside the Grand Divine Uni-Verse
or the One Divine Turning,
my place of Peace and Joy in singularity, this is
my True Divine Holy Family."

I feel this strongly. I "know" this somehow.

*There is an ancient remembrance, a "Holy Knowing"
coming up in and for me.*

And you do not have to leave the Third Dimension to know this; in other words, disincarnate and leave.

The re-remembrance is only ever in the One Mind even when in incarnation.

So do it right wherever you think you are, right now, as the superstar you are.

Once you know who you really are, you can do these sorts of things standing on your head, as they say.

You are indeed brighter than 10,000 stars, in truth.

*And if you are saying "Yes" to these thoughts
and feel that yearning deeper and deeper day by day,
this healing communicating work is for you.*

This yearning is not about looking for a saviour, to save you; it is a fundamental pure desire to recover Holy Family again and join consciously and deliberately to that Holy Family in Holy Knowing.

A return home to Holiness in Knowing.

The Prodigal Child returning from great travels but really only from Virtual Dreamed travels.

*"I am not lost,
I am now found.*

I release the dream."

Know Holiness – this fundamental Truth.

This will nail it down further.

*"Nothing else other than
Divine Singularity is Real or Possible."*

Outside of Reality or Divine Holy Home, it is only possible to Create Virtuality, and those Created Virtualisations are only ever created inside mechanisms inside Holy Reality, that is in the grand halls of the One Mind. Framed as dreams of separation, as mental distortions, as a seemingly lost soul! Conjuring up the virtual with magic.

*"In truth, there is
Nothing Real outside Divine Holy Home"*

You can safely say.

*"Third Dimensional Space with Time,
only resides in the One Mind"*

Without contradiction.

In fact,

*"Third Dimensional Space with Time
exists as an idea, a concept,
a mental projection only in the One Mind".*

And you have done extremely well in the Third-

Dimension virtual metaphorical theatre – creating separation – dualities – great dramas – many belief systems – grand philosophies – intellectual hierarchies – politics with power – religions with beliefs – cults with cultural systems to create meaning, all based in and fuelled by the misperception of body-centric ego energies of Fear, Guilt and Judgements.

> *"All of this is quite meaningless in Holy Home Reality.*
>
> *But holding great value only inside the virtual ego creation of seeming separation."*

Now that is nice to "know"!

So, change is possible and there is something far grander awaiting your decision.

And. of course, this:

> *"This Whole Projected Metaphorical Virtuality*
> *can dissolve and translate*
> *when the value holding it in place is released."*

That is even more amazing.

You have been doing this magic trick regularly in life.

It is called "moving on" and "letting go". I release the need!

You are an expert at this.

> *"This Virtual game of separation will end when the Mental and Emotional Energy holding it all in place is dissolved or let go or released and it becomes of no worth any further*
>
> *With the newfound "Holy Knowing".*

Not Worth-shipped any more.

Yes, that is where that word (worship) came from. Thank you, Jeshua.

And so, I will leave you at this point for more cogitation and reflection of who you really are and with your inner mental yearnings.

Yes, it is only a simple decision to release and move attention to the Holy Singularity of Reality and your grand desire to return Home to being fully aware of your Holiness in Knowing.

Allowing the flow of Holy Karma in your own life.

This is the Mental Zone where you are now placing more and more attention, allowing the Flow of Divine Holy Love itself and the mystery of the Holy Spirit, to wrap you up regularly and assist you to finally slip into Holy Surrender.

To arrive back home as the great traveller that has

gone nowhere, only in dreams. A journey of no distance to a place you never left. Just slight-of-hand stuff.

This is Holy Karma arising. Holiness in Knowing.

The Divine Holy Source (God), The Holy Spirit, and the Children of God are all One, in all possible meanings and ways, as there is only the One (universe).

The Father and I are One
The Father, the Son and the Holy Spirit
and these three are one.
The Mother, the Daughter and the Holy Spirit
and these three are one.
Yes, there is only the "One Holy Divine Expression",
ever or possible.
Yes, you are inside and part of that expression,
"Divine by Birth and Nature.

Holiness in Knowing".

And now in process of opening once again to living in the flow of Holy Karma.

You can also say quite safely, without any contradiction,

"Only God Exists."

Reflect on that.

Last "Holy Knowing".

Are you part of that "Only God Exists" if you exist also?

How connected is that?

Love to all those with Holiness in Knowing.

Love to you all from Shamaré

The Protector
The Door Keeper
The Gatekeeper
The Guardian of the Holy Karma Arising Now

5.
Holy Karma > The Holiness in Decision

It is now time to move to a "Newer Statement on Enlightenment".

Many, over the years, have been given direction and personal guidance from the Ascended Masters and this has led to much advancement towards awakening from ego and illusion.

These early enlightened ones continue to mature, not because the Ascended Masters are teaching them new stuff (what can be new?) but now from their own Holy Awareness Arising.

They are also becoming Arising Masters now.

This new Awareness they have is that "Holiness in Completion" is available to them if they decide personally to step into the Holy Karma Flowing.

> *This deciding without external inputs*
> *is their own "Holiness in Decision".*
> *Deciding brings up the Power*
> *to move through the final Holy Steps*
> *and allow Holy Karma to flow once again.*

*Inside that Personal Decision,
is "Holiness Itself or Holiness in Completion".*

*Only an entity that knows deeply
that they are a Holy Child
could ever decide such a thing.*

Many more will have this Holy Knowing in time.

This chapter will be of assistance to the many already moving forward with "The Healing of their Holy Mind" while seemingly living inside this Domain of Dualities.

This Domain, you now know is only a "Creation or Virtuality", has primary ego beliefs of mental and spatial separation from Divine Holy Source.

Supporting the belief in Divine Separation is the misunderstanding that the souls involved in humanity are only biological DNA animal body forms that have evolved from a swamp somewhere, somehow, at some time.

There are many other equally odd ego misperceptions and illusions supporting the belief in separation.

These beliefs often arise in a soul's mind when entering and then experiences incarnated living in this duality game of virtuality, creations, with DNA bodies.

One of the biggest misunderstandings of being separated from Holy Divinity, is that there is no ability or method to reconnect and close the gap.

That only a powerful saviour could arrange such a thing!

This belief is the driver of many victim thoughts and often mental outcomes with almost a complete loss of connection with the Divine Holy Family.

This big misunderstanding through human ego history has led many to undertake to find a perfect sacrifice as an offering to gaining God's favour once again and be able to return Home.

An appeasement of some type to allow recovery. Even going to the extent of making up a perfect human sacrifice and believing this will fix things.

A correction on this ancient perfect sacrifice ego idea is offered here.

This is, of course, a major mental delusion and a huge mental illusion. Large numbers of humans over eons have fallen into this trap and created many religions around this special sacrifice ego Idea.

Any physical sacrifice is meaningless and worthless, obviously, with what we now know.

> *How could something that is not real*
>
> *have any impact on outcomes in Reality?*

That does mean then that all the sacrificed animals and humans for eons past have achieved nothing at all, as no ego sacrifice can achieve anything, other than this one simple sacrifice.

> *Your own personal sacrifice*
> *of dropping this insane ego deception.*
>
> *Can you sacrifice this idea*
> *to gain Divine Freedom?*

In the depths of ego madness, divine connection might seem faded and even appear to disappear for a while but understand a body sacrifice is not the answer or required, only a simple remembrance and a Holy Decision is required.

The dropping of the madness, as a simple sacrifice to correct an ego misperception.

> *During ego body incarnations*
> *Holiness may seem lost*
> *with ego mind distractions and misperceptions,*
> *to only reappear for you*
>
> *as you move to your own Holiness in Decision.*

You are that powerful, you may not realise this yet!

You can get lost in the human ego mind and DNA body experience and then at some point decide to choose to awaken. Awakening sufficiently to make the required Holy Decision, by dropping the ego mind distraction and, *voilà*, back comes the Holy Connection and the return of the Holy Family, never lost and then the welcome home party.

Play the game and hide the Holy Family connection from yourself, then wave the metaphorical mental miracle hand and the Holy Family reappears, as not lost, just an Illusion, a trick of mind. A master magician at work.

Sort of like losing the car keys, wandering around in a daze for some time, and finding them again by the remembrance of where you last put them.

Hiding inside this Holiness in Decision are amazing mental changes that will arise that lead back to Holiness in Knowing.

Enlightening information on ways to rectify these ego misperceptions comes to all progressively, yes, but it does come, even if it seems like a forever wait. Call out for help!

Some will have to wait quite a time yet, due to deep madness and stubbornness.

There are no other possible outcomes

> as Reality Home can never be lost forever.
>
> I release the need to feel I have lost connection!
>
> And, of course, the need holding you back
> is the cause also.
> Find the cause and the need evaporates!
>
> It is wholly self-created, probably ancient!
>
> Sacrifice it on your own altar.

So, you are very safe always, even when you feel victim, lost, unloved, no hope and abandoned.

To heal a mind of these "faulty ego belief systems" that is feeling and believing they are separated, lost, forgotten, abandoned, with no hope and more can be a challenge.

It requires a turning around in the seat of the soul, driven by great longing for True Holy Family again.

> "One part of the Holy Decision
> is to develop a greater dedication to Holy Self."
> This makes all the difference.
>
> It is called Self Love or Holy Self Love.

Here is a thought to assist those choosing Holiness in Decision with dedication and longing.

> You can only have arisen from Divinity Itself,
> yes, and that Divinity is imbued in you, never to be lost.

Your Consciousness Arises from this Divinity.

Your Awareness is rooted strongly in this Holy Family.

Sit inside that thought for a while; it may overwhelm you.

*Yes, and furthermore,
also now know that the original decision
to birth you as Holy Spirit Child,*

was made out of deep Holy Love.

Note: Body DNA is only a metaphorical mimic of

*"Your True Holy DNA,
that is the unbroken intertwined
Holy Family's Spiritual Helix relationship
in multiple dimensions,*

with All as the One Divine Body."

The Holiness in Decision is now brewing in many, bubbling away, even frothing.

As more difficult ego human duality events unfold, what now arises correspondingly in the many, arising from old original memory with imagination, is this great longing, the great crying out, for the "close Divine Holy Family bond" once again, seemingly lost so long ago. Remembrance, imagination, like the children's story books.

Do not despair over Earth, World and Human Turmoil. The meek will inherit the Earth.

> "I now desire my True Holy Divine Family
> More than All Other Things".

Say it, just to try it on. It will bubble away in many forms, watch it and sigh,

> "I do remember."
> "I choose to remember more fully."
> "I open myself to more memories."
> I release the need to have thoughts of separation,
> I weep and tremble in anticipation
> of my Holy Home coming,
> awakening from ego slumber,
> full of dreams of separation,
>
> with fears, guilts and judgements.

So let us move from this stirring introduction for this chapter and focus more words, to feed your personal dedication and longing.

Let's grow your Holiness in Decision. Some advice to start:

> "Your new spiritual practice of patiently
> and diligent watching your ego mind activity,
> so as to catch your own mental ego reactivities,
>
> is of most importance at this pivotal time".

You only ever see your own belief system reflecting and these beliefs can be released.

Time is not standing still in the 3D Space Virtual Creation but moving inexorably to several conclusion markers and a final turning point.

The many markers are things like more ego-minded human strife and with many more living difficulties arising, as the proposed ego solutions slowly lose power and collapse, as they will indeed.

The final turning point is arriving for humanity to make the Holiness in Decision.

Will you make it? There is no judgement if you don't at this time but just more ongoing incarnations living in dualities in another Domain somewhere until you are prepared to awaken and Love yourself enough again.

This decision is driven by your base desires and Self-Love.

The final turning point will come for earth, world and humanity, yes, a miracle, a change is coming in the earth world human outcomes, from what looked so devastated and lost and impossible at present.

The Miracle arising from the many Holiness in Decisions

is Heaven on Earth, where we the meek
(Holiness in Decision makers)
will finally be able to anchor ourselves mentally
in Holy Peace and Joy, even inside a virtuality.
These meek ones will be wrapped
in the framework of Holy Karma once again.
A full remembrance of the Holy Family
has taken place for these ones.

A returning home
of the Prodigal Cosmic travelling Holy Child.

And so, the outcome for the Holy Awakening will be of a personal nature for each Holy Child, with variations tailored to their circumstances, mentally and emotionally.

That must feel good!?

Here is a short look at how this can come true for the many.

Questions arise in minds often and even in human sleep dreams can be answered and minds can be healed.

Who am I really?
Who am I right now?
What is my purpose?
Why am I suffering?
Where do I look for solutions?
Are there solutions?
Should I fact check this?

What am I meant to believe?
Are beliefs useful?

*The answers and actions to these
and many other questions you decide upon
will decide your mental progress
and mental healing may follow that
Holiness in Decision.*

Your Holiness in Decision will always be the lead for you.

Decide carefully for yourself, only inside Holy Self Love. Do this when you feel Peaceful and in Joy.

If your answers and decisions are to continue the human ego experiences, misperceptions, misidentification, that says, "I am only body, just DNA, just Jim or Mary standing here and not Spirit or a Holy Child", then there will be no mental progress and the internal ego mental fight will continue and manifest itself over and over again as the "transmutation of Divine Love" takes place in your ego mind.

This will lead to more doubt, madness and confusion with no true direction, often circular arguments in the mind that stall any progress and mental healing.

*A revisiting of old haunts (concepts)
in new sets of clothes.*

> *The walking of the same valley track*
> *with different eyes (other incarnations),*
>
> *hoping to see and find something new*
> *that will sort it out.*

Or as one said long ago,

> *"As a dog returning to its vomit."*

Harsh indeed but apt. Going back for another look at ego misperception once again!

Consider carefully, take your time, do not rush into faulty pathways, stop associating with people that could beguile you. In fact, find new friends to encourage you.

Open your Holy Self to prompting from the Holy Spirit that will assist Holy Karma to come into your Life.

> *I desire to shift and change my mind on many things.*
> *I feel this, I am not comfortable*
> *in my present mind's state.*
>
> *This Holy Cause driving the desire. Self-Love!*

This is a good start point, letting emotions be the guides, not intellect now.

> *"I choose to open to what I know is true!"*
> *I release the need to not know about*
> *Holiness any further.*

Again, this Holy Cause driving the desire. Self-Love!

Others may laugh at your plan, so courage is required.

It is my Holiness in Decision and I will choose for my Holy Self now!

> *"I am fundamentally Spirit, a Holy Child.*
> *I open my communications to the invisible*
> *once again in Trust.*
> *I release the need to feel lost and unloved.*

Again, this Holy Cause driving the desire. Self-Love!

This may seem a little strange, especially if you think you are a so-called intellectual or trying to be rational (has it helped?). Open anyway. That ongoing mental storm in your ego mind is your prompt to turn aside and use the old ideas and patterns to heal your mind. Continual thinking does not fix this.

The receiving of the energy of Divine Love Flowing from the Holy Spirit supports and enlivens all souls and can seemingly extend into this physical creation, via your Holy Mind.

> *"Love flows to you and through you,*
> *not from a source apart from you*
> *but from a Holy Source in the very depth of you,*
> *from Divine Holy Family*

in the form of the Holy Spirit."

You have been given the freedom to use this Holy Energy as you will it, and many in humanity have decided to distort it with their own powerful mental ego trans-mutations, into created projections of dualities, that are wrapped in Fears, Guilts and Judgements resulting in great insanity. Sound familiar?

Hence the confusion and the difficulty and the duality fights, for who is right and who is wrong, who has the power, who is cancelled etc. Ignore it all.

In the mental process of creating Dualities to live in and to fight inside of, there develops "Complexity upon complexity", which only the Priests of this World are able to explain what it is all about and what it is all for. Resulting in everyone becoming more entrapped and powerless. They will mandate you to conform, cancel you if you don't. Be cancelled, who needs their thoughts?

> "Ego intellectual answers are the driving force
> into more madness." The history!
> And included in that madness
> is the "Ignoring of inner prompting
> by Spirit, your own Holiness", that says so often,
> "Child awaken, it is only your creation,
> it is only a dream, not Reality,

you are in ego virtual projection."

You volunteered remember, door 23.
You are tricking yourself again!

You know all of this well, brush it aside and choose Holiness in Decision.

And so, any thoughts that arise outside this simple truth,

"I am Spirit fundamentally, a Holy Child, loved eternally, unchanged, unchanging, unchangeable."

will continue to cause great upheavals in each person's life, as mental aberration, even sometimes spilling off into the physical due to poor choices.

Yes, the body will mimic the mental via faulty projections of the mind.

This ego misperception struggle has caused the process of creating great belief systems that are an attempt to mimic "True Reality Flowing", with the inevitable downside of never fulfilling the desires hoped for.

"Human Duality Belief Systems will all fail eventually,
leading to the feeling of loss and hopelessness
and even more separation",
often leading to the creating of
newer complex belief systems
that further entrap, beguile and disappoint.

Human ego systems now are ready to implode under the weight of discontent and in-fighting that is developing inside all world systems.

How, then, to make the great escape from ego misidentification?

If you are prepared to become an observer of these ego misidentifications, and you can, you will find that all of the arising mental reactivity, conflict, confusion, projection, emotion, disturbance, can be used as your awakening cue cards, your personal signals to self, an internal mental flag prompting you to move to healing, because you have fooled yourself once again, falling into "the unnatural ego world filled with Fear, Judgement and Guilt".

This can only ever be true, as

*"Denial of the flow of the Holy Spirit in your life
only leads to more and more distortion
by ego mind and with ego actions."*

Moving away from your goal of Holiness

It is of course only the process of circling around and falling once again into the unnatural, hoping for a different outcome in delusion, once again.

*However, know this:
even in the most extreme of mental distortions
and endless ego circles,*

*that is the Trans-mutating of Divine Natural Holy Love
to fear and confusion,
you are safe and loved, as you live out your illusions
in a dreamlike insane state.
Inside that framework it is still possible
to reach up and choose again
and then arise again.*

*Know you are fundamentally sound,
unchanged in Holiness.*

The correction for the delusion is only that Holiness in Decision away, to an allowing of change to arise in the mind. I release the need to be lost now. The need, of course, is the tricking of yourself over and over, to feel lost. Probably very old.

A listening to the inner mental prompting and allowing Holy Spirit finally to come through the dream, the deep slumber, the faulty illusion with the awakening prompting to see the light of your Divine Holy Nature.

Like a tunneller escaping from a prison, digging in darkness with great hope and then, there it is, the opening with the light and freedom.

Keep digging!

"Know this, worldly power is an illusion of ego body mind, inside the mental distortion, inside the mental factory of transmutation of Divine Love Flowing", with ego fear, guilt and judgment.

All that seek this type of power always fail, always, never succeeding in the long search for the

Peace and Joy of Holy Mind,

always beyond human ego understanding and comprehension."

This awaits and resides in the Divine Cupboard of your Holy Mind. How could ego ever understand this?

And so, it is this way for All, until the Holiness in Decision is made and with that decision finally:

Allow, Trust and Embrace your own
"ego creations of mental distortion",
by allowing the healer,
that is "Divine Holy Love Flowing",
now unimpeded as Pure Divine Healing Energy.

Only Holy Love heals all things!

Allowing Holy Karma to arise in your Holy Mind. Healing cannot be achieved any other way.

Your ego mind cannot be magically fixed/ transformed inside ego mental distortion, inside the ego misidentification, full of ego misperception or ego learning.

It is a very good idea to heal yourself from these ego illusions as rapidly as you can.

Remember this, the results of ego mental distortion are as a projected creation, hence the reflected insanity, the madness, believing it is all true and only true or possible.

Anything outside the Divine (God)

can only be a Mimic, a Creation, never the Reality.

And by the way, just in case you have forgotten.

"Only God Exists", "The All", "The One" and therefore that is why

*"**Only Love is Real**".*

Always totally true and you are an Integral Part of that One, the Loving Divine Holy Family.

Everything else ego humanity thinks is real inside in ego duality; it is just a mental aberration.

It is as a creation and doesn't really exist, other than as a dream in an ego mind and not in the Reality of the Divine Mind itself, herself, himself, the Self.

Hence, throughout time, some have had a Holy Revelation when listening to the invisible, their Holy Self.

One of these, many years ago, had realisations on impermanence (temporary, passing, brief, fleeting, elusive, mortal, short-lived, flying, fugitive, transient, momentary, ephemeral, transitory, perishable etc.).

We have now amplified that ancient concept thought, many times over now, with purer Divine Holy Knowing.

And so, once you have passed this hurdle of ego misidentification, True Power comes and that Flow returns with the embracing of Spirit.

The embracing brings forth a Holy Mental Transformation and with it a "New Holy You" will arise from the ash heap of mental distortion. A Holy Mental trans-cendance happens with the thought and a new viewpoint.

> "I am not the created DNA body.
>
> I am fundamentally Spirit only and always".

That is it; the Holiness in Decision is made.

At last.

You have always been there, just hidden away some of the time.

I have not cursed God and died (Spiritually). I sat in the ash heap in sack clothes and waited for healing to come for me. I decided this, I decided this, this is my Holiness in Decision, this is my life, this is my new direction, I am returning home to my Holy Family again, after great mental travelling and pain.

Thank Heavens, there is still a door open for me to slide through!

Actually, you never left; who needs a door?

You have tried all sort of ego contrivances to rise above the disillusionment, but to no avail.

They may work for a while, being busy, busy in learning, busy in making money, making, making but it all comes to an end at some point when your mental failures finally create a point in time of despair.

Finally, a little quietness arises where, at last, "The small voice of reason" says,

"My Holy Child, it is time,
it is your time now, move to allow the flow of Holy Love,
move to heal your Mental Distortion,
and finally turn off your transmutation
of the Divine Holy Love Flowing."

Allow Holy Karma to rule your life.

It has been all hard work, with no pay cheque, just distortion.

Make that Holiness in Decision.

> *"And there you are,
> reborn it would seem, as from Holy Spirit,
> but not really, you have always been Spirit in Nature*
>
> *but by now you know this, you feel this very deeply."*

You return to the way it has always been without illusion, just the simplicity of Holy Divinity in singularity.

> *"The Prodigal Cosmic Holy Child returning home to great celebrations."*

And with the return to Holy Home comes the most outstanding revelation and encouragement for you.

The Law of Holy Love does not sit on top of any human belief systems: a religion, a philosophy, a culture, any other thing.

It stands by itself as the

> *"Foundation Stone of your Existence",*
>
> *arising from the Singular Point
> of Holy Consciousness that you are.*

The simplicity of all of this is lost with the busyness of the ego, the body-centric mind.

The scurrying.

Yes, you are always OK, just stop distorting your True Holy Nature.

Choose your words to represent the Real Holy You now.

With the predominance of Flow of Divine Love again (non-mutated), there is an arising of power, true Power.

This Power is unassailable by any ego body mind. Love is the Uni-verse's Holy Power.

You are now in safe territory, Heaven on Earth.

Holy Karma running.

> *"You need not defend or validate yourself any further to anyone, with words or deeds."*

This Arising of Holy Karma now flows through you, as you become the

> *"Great Effect for the Divine itself".*

This of course, all arises nowhere but in your mind, from the very depth of you, down to the depths of Divinity (God) itself.

Yes, you are connected to Divinity itself, you always have been, there is no separation, it was a mental hoax you played on yourself.

It is not possible to disconnect, you are part of the One, the ALL, the Universe, the "Uni", one, the "Verse", turning, the one turning, there is only one thing.

How could it be any other way, you must be Divine and Holy to be able to appreciate and know what is happening inside the awakening and keep going in that direction, not turning aside.

Remembrance is putting on of a new set of legs (members) on the Holy Beginnings once again. I do know this; how?

It would be impossible to know and understand this Holy Healing Process if you do not have the comprehension inside your mind already.

This knowing exists in All.

It is there before you thought you were lost.

Hence your great yearning for connection with the Divine Family again, a remembrance arising of the Holy family that you were birthed into; yes, your True Holy Family.

And the beauty of all of this, even in Third Dimension virtuality, is that it is natural and requires no schooling, no belief, no culture, no books and only a little intellect, no politics, religion or philosophy for you to become aware of this.

Just an opening of your emotional mind to the possibility once again and making your Holiness in Decision.

> *"I decide today and always."*

No saviour is required either, unless you would like to have one for a little while, until you are strong enough to stand on your own two spiritual Holy feet.

If having a saviour gives you, as an awakening child, some strength it is OK. However, it is just another illusion, that is not a requirement.

You can let this saviour belief go also when you feel it is time, as you are the Holy Saviour of the world now.

You have now reached "Bedrock", you have reached Solidity (Reality), you can now embrace all of creation itself without prejudice (judgement), fear or guilt and with full knowing that all creation can pass away at the whim of the Divine Energy that holds it in place.

This is how sure you can become, and you remain safe always.

They will say Christ is with us again.

And it is true, a Christ Mind walking the earth once again. The second coming at last.

Madness ends, Love arises.

Tranquillity is suspended once again inside a Joyous Mind, now fully opened to the Divine Flow of Love, without resistance or need of modification. Holy Karma at work.

A little more for you, because there is always another question.

For some, this Holy Arising will not come in time for them to move into this current domain's arising Heaven on Earth.

They will stubbornly not make the Decision in Holiness inside the present Holy Time frame.

These will have to change domains, move neighbourhoods as it has been said so many times, without any divine judgement, so as to continue the process of moving towards Enlightenment, at some other point in another duality domain, inside that domain's created time.

All, wherever they are, will eventually heal and reach into the Holiness of Decision and allow Holy Karma to flow and become again, the effect of Holy Spirit itself, always and forever.

> *So please, "Do not waste time",*
> *but use time constructively always,*
>
> *watching the mind*
> *for arising distortions to be healed.*

Jeshua Ben Joseph's plea from many years back. (He actually said, "Waste not, another moment.")

Heed the arising moments in your mind, do not throw them away as disposables but see them as of great value, your treasure and always ask if healing is required for this misperception.

You are only bringing them forward for your own healing; it would not happen otherwise.

If you find you are bound and stuck by political or culture or religion or philosophy or intellectual beliefs that slow and maybe stop your progress, *dump them and move on.*

> "As a Holy Self in search mode, driven by desire."

Do not look back, like the wife of Lot, and do forget the things behind.

In fact, as you heal the moments, they will not be there to reflect on any more.

They will be evaporated and are gone, as creations always do when motivation and value (energy) is removed.

> *"The Dumping" of limiting things, my friends,*
> *is a requirement.*

> *You cannot serve two Masters.*

Sometimes it is very painful and disconnecting and at times seems like agony, with more mental distortion arising as those precious false beliefs fight to be recognised, crying out for just one more recognition.

And the answer,

> *"Get behind me Satan, your day has passed."*

Not that Satan is a person but is a strong

> *"Psychological ego force in any disturbed ego mind"*

> *that demands its voice and role*
> *as leader and decider in your ego life.*

However, you have made your Holiness in Decision, you are the Chooser now, not the belief, the culture, the religion, the philosophy, the ego, not any modality.

You are now the Holy Master of the Decide.

All these ego things are but trifles for the awakened Holy Mind, as it knows that

> *"All the beliefs rest on no rock foundation, but sand."*
>
> *"Beliefs are a very faulty weak attempt to replicate Holy Home."*

They float in space, as illusion, built on sand and will pass away when you turn your back on them and walk away. They drop and dissolve and are gone forever.

So, inside your agony, see and appreciate that this Holiness in Decision has come for you, either you move to heal misperception or you fall back into contamination and distortion once again.

> *"Sort of like giving up any addiction really."*

Great courage is required to shake all of this off, and eventually it will come with Holy Joy.

> *"I shake you (thing, belief, distortion, illusion, madness) off in Holy Joy"*
>
> and it is done.

The reason:

> *"I desire to see and to feel Holy Peace arising, coming with Holy Joy."*

Holy Karma reigns supreme in a healed mind and it is enough.

Peace flows easily inside this Reality itself, with the mental ego fight gone at last.

So, your Holiness in Decision is for yourself now.

This moment, any moment (is the right now), and is critical for your Holy Awakening to come.

Choose > Holy Love Flowing
Choose > Holy Karma allowing Divine Will
Choose >The Flow of Holy Spirit once again in purity, with no distortion of that energy.

Holy Spirit is the "Composite Loving Energy of all residing inside Holy Karma".

Yes, a new definition.

A little more encouragement for you.

Are you one of the Holy Children?

Without any doubt
All are the Children of the Divine
Even other types of souls

otherwise none would exist.

Nothing exists outside Holiness.

Love to all the Holiness Deciders.

Love to you all from Shamaré

The Protector
The Door Keeper
The Gatekeeper
The Guardian of the Holy Karma Arising Now

6.
Holy Karma > Holiness Arising

How does the framework of Holy Karma arrive in a Holy Mind that once believed it was an ego body mind, with misidentification as a DNA human body named Jim or Mary?

This is called the process of "Holiness Arising".

Holy Karma arrives and arises progressively in each Holy Mind as they "mentally realign Identification with True Holy Spirit Self" once again.

This is "Holiness Arising".

It is an entirely "Natural Process, without learning, only requiring a dedication, a longing, a decision, an allowance, a surrender and the choice to be found and made inside the Holiness of the One Mind".

"Holiness Arising is the means to bring Heaven to Earth."
"Holiness is the natural outcome of an Arising in an awakening Holy Mind."

"Holiness Arising is Holy Karma in flow."

Holy Cause driving Holy Effect.

Allow this process.

Holiness Arising is a Holy Function controlled by your decision, in contrast to an ego decision that leads to a disconnection from Holiness, a seemingly holiness declining.

You are the Holy Pilot always.

*And so, without Holiness Arising
inside the flow of Holy Karma,
the old ego misidentification order continues
until "The Holy Release
and The Holy Decision
and The Holy Choice"
is made by the many to join the*

*"Natural Flow of Holy Love" once again,
without distorting or mutating it any longer.*

That process is forgetting the things behind and moving into a new mental realm. The Holy Mental Surrender of "not my will be done but thine". An alignment with Holiness once again. The Holy Natural order.

This Holiness Arising is to be achieved even while inside incarnation in the "earth world human creation" by the Holy Minds that now know they dwell in Reality only.

As this Holy Arising (seemingly inside a Creation) is

a great surprise to many and not really expected. Holiness is usually inside Reality and of course that is where it is Arising but manifesting in creation.

It is metaphorical, this new Holy Realm Arising, outside reality manifesting in creation.

Often called a New Heaven and a New Earth.

This Arising Holiness is a mental state that is allowed and is never limited to a specific location somewhere.

Heaven = Love Flowing inside a Mind at Peace, in any domain, in a Mind that only knows thoroughly that "Only Holy Love is Real".

Operating as True Holy Self:

> *"I am but Spirit"*
>
> *as the Holy Child of the Divine Itself.*

A return of a Holy One, not that it was ever lost, only just imagined lost or dreamed lost.

And there you have it, the

> *"Flow of Holy Love emboldens"*
>
> *all those moving into Holy Karma*
> *to effortlessly Arise in Holiness.*

A new era of Holiness manifested into a created

form, maybe for the second time, but this time in the form of Spirits incarnating as human beings. Amazing. The second coming of Christ itself, that is Christ mind or the Holy Mind on earth again. Yes, that is the second coming; Jeshua is not coming back to earth. You can plead but he is not coming. It is our opportunity now.

A Holy Creation, a projection of Holy Mind, that is "Heaven on Earth".

*The "Holiness Arising flowing out as Holy Karma"
will come only if and only when
the "Holy Decision and Choice
to Identify with being fundamentally Spirit"*

is fully realised and actualised.

*This "Full Realisation and Actualisation"
is not a learning process,
as in books, but a learning as in "experiential only".
Actualising is walking the talk
and it will be very obvious to all.*

They will call you Emmanuel!

The complete surrender of the ego mind must take place.

This arrives by internal Divine Holy Communion (Holy Spirit), with allowing, trusting, embracing, all feelings, emotions, insight, questions, projections, contemplation and then surrendering ego.

Holy Awareness Arises inside the trials and tribulations of the ego mind where the fight for supremacy between ego karmic mind and Holy Karmic mind is finally struggled out. Not that there is any doubt on the outcome.

Struggle and fighting not literally but moment by moment in a healing Awakening Holy Mind until the ego is finally laid to rest, as a valueless item that needs to be discarded. A piece of madness.

This is the way of Holiness Arising, to allow Holy Karma to flow fully and continually inside an awakened Holy Mind.

A progressive expansion of Awareness occurs.

"I am that and more yet!"

And what would you say in this "Moment of Holiness Arising"?

Exclamations of

*Praise God for the gift of
Consciousness and Holy Awareness, life itself.
Dualities banished, judgement, fear and guilt gone
as if not ever having existed, now forgotten.
Like old ideas, of no value, deleted!*

or

Praise Divine Oneness, where **"Only Love is Real"**.

or

*Praise the Holy Spirit
which is the Holy Bridge back to Holy Home.*

*All being quite applicable for you
at that time of Holiness Arising.*

*"A falling to your knees in gratitude"
for your Holy Recovery.*

"I am healed of ego misperception."

"I Am now Holy Me and I know this!"

Holy Knowing.

Holiness Arises from Purity of Holy Love, without any judgement, held in perfect union with the Holy Spirit.

Pure Holy Sanity again:

The Father, the Son and the Holy Spirit
The Mother, the Daughter and the Holy Spirit
The Divine, the Holy Children and the Holy Spirit}

And these three are all one as the Divine Mystery of consciousness and awareness.

All of the same Holy Family.

Arising from the Grand Intelligence, the single point of Consciousness.

And so, my dear friends, do not waste another moment in sorting all of this out in your Holy Mind.

Do make the Holy Decision to move into the New Earth, The New Jerusalem, a New Creation.

> *"There will be Holy Ones arising from the north, the south, the east and the west. to join you."*

> *"The New Format for expressing Holy Love Again in Fullness"*

> *even inside a creation, a miracle!*

Inside this new format, the incarnated Holy Family lives and dwells in perfect union with the Holy Spirit, all now acting in the image of the begetting Divine Single Source of Consciousness.

Replicators of Pureness, Holiness with Divine Love Flowing effortlessly inside the non-constricting Singularity of Holy Energy.

Pure Holy Karma in action, the Holy Divine Cause and the Holy Divine Effect moving quietly and powerfully over the surface of the deep, the Holy Mind.

Holiness Arising is the only subject and purpose in

the minds of those surrendering and falling into Holy Karma.

A little to ponder on.

*Holiness may be something you may
not have considered until now.*

*Holiness is you in singularity itself,
with only Divine Love Flowing.*

Allow this Holiness to Arise in your mind.

That is enough on Holiness Arising for this moment, more is coming, as we move from these very dark days to days of full light, with many now realising and aching for that Day to come.

A little caution for you.

Many, in mental belief distortion, would like to see the old ego karma healed and for it to become Holy, but alas this is misguided and foolish in the minds of the Holy Ones.

*Many talk as if this is possible.
"Believe me and Trust me",
turn and dust the sandals once again.
Many plans, many meetings and much discussion.*

*However, Holiness cannot arise inside
non-Holiness or ego misidentification.*

The Real Solution.

A turning of the head to new (ancient) things is required for new (ancient) beginnings. (Time is not here.)

There will be days of despondency and regrets but know that Heaven on Earth does not arise from non-holy.

> *Many are trying to use the intellect to turn*
> *the ego around from madness and tyranny*
> *but it is only ever into a new madness, always.*
> *Many may start talking of systems*
> *that do acts of kindness,*
> *but it just to beguile, to ruin,*
> *to corrupt and mislead.*

> *Put a large mental distance between yourself*
> *and any voice saying these types of things.*

Turn the eyes and head away, block the ears, dust off the sandals, and walk to another village, where Holiness Arising is now showing itself.

If you are among the many feeling lost and abandoned in this old world and are aching to see

"Change in a Holy Way come",

now is your time to move and do not look back.

Disconnect from ego-world propaganda now.

> *"Those who do not teach that*

"Only Love is Real"
are to be ignored now.

Turn the back and mentally walk away.

Allow the Holy Spirit to move your feet, your heart and mind and walk or run to your new Holy Family as Holiness Arising flowing Holy Karma.

I am returning home.

*"Become the Divine Effect
to co-create the new Heaven on Earth,*

as Holiness Arising."

A Holy Projection.

*So, be among the "Achers",
be "among the Righteous at Heart",
be "among the Holy Karma Family Arising",
become the meek (the Allowers, the Surrenders).*

Contemplate well what is before you, not necessarily just the words but the evoking of feeling arising in you.

You will be propelled as you realise that the Holy Love flowing is actually your own Holy Self Love once again.

It arises from inside Holiness, and projects through as Holy Effect, without ego Transmutation.

A letting it be Pure Holiness this time.

Not tainted or muddled in dualities.

Are you in great desire to move now, into Holy Karma, are you aching for change?

Allow these feelings coming through now to be healed; weep inside this and smile.

Even if it does require a new incarnation. You will remember.

> *Refocus your Attention and Intention.*
>
> *Trust the Holy Spirit to lead you through
> this transition and distracting time.*
>
> *This is a time of much injustice and corruption
> as the ego goes completely insane
> to retain and gain power.*
>
> *It is not the first time that humanity
> has had to lived inside of this,
> but it will be the last time.*

As we move deeper into the book with greater Holiness in Knowing, the resulting discussions will become more and more obvious and therefore fewer words will be devoted to the subject and the focus will move to feeling rather than thinking.

This is only natural, as the end state is not words, only feeling and peace with Joy.

Allow the next few closing chapters to guide you into this Holy Mental state by allowing and surrendering into Holy Spirit as it finally finds a new home permanently with you.

Love to all the Holy Deciders with Arising Holiness.

Love to you all from Shamaré

The Protector
The Door Keeper
The Gatekeeper
The Guardian of the Holy Karma Arising Now

7.
Holy Karma > Holiness in Self Love

Holy Self Love is the first of the many Holy Karma mental facilities that start opening like the petals of a flower, even well before you recognise your Holiness Journey has started. An early spring bloom.

This also will often be the case, even before you are aware that there is a Holy Process, a Holy Curriculum to work through. As in spring, the natural urge to bloom will arise even before the warmth.

Even ego intellectual (unemotional) decisions will often lead to the start of Holy Awareness opening, the beginning of the arise of Holiness in Self Love.

Misidentified ego often in desperation will start looking for "other" solutions to ego life's problems and finally turn to:

> "Maybe the subject of spirituality has answers"

not being aware that this is the beginning of the path home.

That looking at spirituality is often opened to find a new tool to sort out ego irritations and world-incarnated human power issues, not Holiness.

A common modality used for the process of sorting out issues is meditation.

> *"Just let me sit in the darkness of my wardrobe for an hour to gain insight and peace!"*

Another modality is the idea of living in mind-fullness.

> *"Let me be mindful of my actions
> and be more Loving
> and compassionate
> as I go through my daily human life!"*

And so, what starts to arise inside these endeavours is the energy of Holy Self Love.

Just maybe, if I do more yoga and meditation, it will all come right, mentally and emotionally, and my perception of life may turn around?!

The next step is becoming aware that there is something else in the wings waiting.

This thought may arise.

*I have done this meditation now for years
but I am still reactive,*

with the same many unanswered questions.

Just sitting hoping.

These thoughts may be the clue you are looking to start awakening and healing your mind. Don't miss these moments; grab them.

Or I still get depressed, now and then

and why?

A sort of organic natural Self Love process starts to occur, out of curiosity.

Everything is not as you would like it to be, there is distortion that manifests itself in viewpoints that often arise from the beliefs, the culture or the religion.

A thought like this may arrive in your mind:

*Maybe I just need to open more
and notice my feelings
and my surroundings' energies more!
Spend more time with nature,
the plants and the animals*

and loving humans.

This is a form of seeking peace of mind which is a precursor to Holy Self Love.

Be careful of virtue signalling, at this point. Remain simple.

It is often the desire just for this simplicity to arise. Just keeping it all simple.

Oh yes, no rules, no rituals, no methods now. Not trying to invoke change, but just allowing.

No Magic. Stay inside Holy Allowing.

The arising of Holiness in Self Love, in simplicity.

And it is all by these simple miraculous start points, happening invisibly inside the mind of one who is aching for Holy Peace and Holy Joy again, even if they do not know that it is possible or exists.

Yes, your desire drives the process, in fact it is Holy Desire. Because you are a Holy Child.

Your honesty and transparency are now opening doors to the invisible and you start letting it in. Yes, really.

"Holy Spirit is always looking for Mental Openings to quietly add support

and new possibility thoughts".

Don't discount this, just open to it, now seeing these as true events in your life.

Allow yourself to be directed; you will arrive at the right time with the right people, so accept this.

This will become your Holy Life. Accept this new life.

Starting to trust the Holy Invisible once again.

It may seem strange at first. How can this possibly be happening? You will grow used to this and then seek it out always.

> *Do not become superstitious about this*
> *and say all sorts of silly things*
> *about your newfound awareness,*
> *making statements like,*
> *I must be one of the favoured ones etc,*
>
> *being all wise around others.*

Just be joyful that Holy Change is now come for you, you can feel it and recognise it in yourself and no formal classes or learning is required, just opening with desire as a flower seeking light.

Also, do not feel somehow you are so special when this occurs.

This is an entirely natural phenomenon and available freely to all, with no specialness.

It is how it is always, in the mental state of Holiness, living in Holiness in Self Love.

This is the beginnings of Holy Karma flowing.

You are not becoming a personal saviour for many yet, just yourself.

Although you may become the saviour of the world in a metaphorical way, as your mind heals.

Some examples of arising Holiness in Self Love.

A small idea arises in the mind. "I am not interfacing with people well, as I approach them, I start judging by appearance, or I am not forming a relationship with them that is loving.

Interesting, I will watch myself from now on and start healing that one as soon as I see it arising.

A decision to stop working in that most horrible of jobs is reflecting Holiness in Self Love.

The leaving of a relationship that became so toxic, beyond recovery, is reflecting Holiness in Self Love.

Just waking up one day with a clear thought,
"I am sure there is much more to my life than this",

is reflecting Holiness in Self Love.

Walking out of any environment that requires an

abnormal unhealthy mental conformity is reflecting Holiness in Self Love.

Finally breaking free from quoting other people's opinions and words as your truths is reflecting Holiness in Self Love. I must therefore stop quoting Jeshua to try to make a point.

> *I release the need to quote Jeshua Ben Joseph. Ha. He keeps whispering in my ear.*

Putting away that Holy Book with all that stuff in it, that you think you live by, is reflecting Holiness in Self Love. It may be difficult at first but give it a go. A peaceful mind will come up as you drop the proscriptions and efforts of faith. It is the simple personal divine experience that you are looking for.

How about this one?

Staying in a relationship that has become so toxic, until you are sure you are clear, and only reflecting Holiness in Self Love and not projecting in to it, causing more toxicity.

> *You have been called to Holy Mental Freedom,*
>
> *not ego world mind conformity.*

Reflect your Holiness as an individual in your Self Love.

Your Holy Power will only arise as you align once again with Holy Divinity, in Singularity.

There are no other possibilities that actually will work. We are talking about True Reality.

It is a choice-less choice; Jeshua again. He gets upset if I break copyright! But think about those words, they are so true, it is purely natural, if you are a Holy Child. There is no other choice!

Many opportunities will arise for you to expand your Holiness in Self Love.

Maybe you are sitting at the dentist's reception and you pick up a magazine with an article that challenges some strongly held belief and it triggers you to do a full Internet search and then you make the change, not to a new belief but the letting go of the old ones. Shed beliefs as unneeded, just more chains to hold you back. Thank heavens I reacted and found that emotional hook! I must go to the dentist more often!

This is reflecting Holiness in Self Love.

Sorting it all out. Move to simplicity.

Drop the need to be right. Who really cares? Only those that want to be right! Find the need's value and drop it.

The "ego need" will be the driving ego cause.

Ask what is driving my need to be right.

> *Drop a lot of stuff.*
> *Drop beliefs that are not required*
> *and there are loads of them.*
> *List six for yourself.*
> *Then drop them.*
> *If you find yourself expounding them again,*
> *just say in correction,*
> *"You know I don't have that belief any more.*
>
> *It is just a nonsense."*
> *Holiness in Self Love healing all things.*

Drop the chains of the past, stop dragging along a whole heap of old reactive remembered stuff holding you back that is zapping your emotional and mental energy.

Awakening from sleep after a dream, and having a realisation that change is needed, is reflecting Holiness in Self Love.

> *Maybe a repeating terrifying dream indicates*
> *something needs to be released.*
> *This is a great act of Holy Self Love.*
>
> *Loving yourself, it will make all the difference.*
>
> *Dreams are invariably about self!*

Apologising to a friend that you may have judged is reflecting Holiness in Self Love.

You decouple yourself from the judgement, inside and out.

Enjoying yourself and laughing and smiling is reflecting Holiness in Self Love.

And, of course, these things are very obvious.

However, no one may have told you that this above is Holiness in Action.

All this indicates to you, you were made and designed to be Joyful, Peaceful in Mind and have strong Self Love and live with the perfect understanding you are free always.

These are the divine rights and gifts bestowed upon you when you were begotten out of Holiness as a Spirit entity, begotten in Holy Love.

This will never change; it is sealed for eternity.

And now for some things that are not even noticed as acts of Holiness in Self Love.

These may seem frivolous.

The decision to buy new clothes or shoes.

This is not addressed to the shopaholics that get an

ego buzz. However, even these shoppers love the mimic feeling of almost Joy that runs through them somewhere, until they are not fashionable.

All of the desire for peace and joy are built into the Holy Mind from Ancient Memory. (Yes, you were there.)

Taking a shower, enjoying it
and feeling it all over the body
and then saying out loud, yes, do it.

"I am actually experiencing
all of those feelings in the shower,
in my Holy Mind only,
Inside Reality itself, where I exist always.

Did you get that?
Sit in that realisation.

"That is where it is felt."
Your Holy Mind, yes.
Only ever possible in the Holy Mind,
this is how close you are to Holiness always.
Every day you sit inside the Holy Mind using its function.
Allow this mind to run in Holiness for you
without you distorting it.

Let it free-wheel and flow out.
Know this clearly, that all feelings are only
ever appreciated in the Spiritual Holy Domain,
in the One Mind, not in the body.
The connection to divinity is that close always.

Jeshua says closer than the width of a thought.

*Reach out and touch this
Divinity as Holiness in Self Love.
Marvel at that! Weep about this. Know this.
Actualise this. Each time.*

*Pinch your body and say the same thing.
Keep that virtuality disclosure thought
in your Holy Mind.
That is how close the incarnated connection and
experience is to Divinity.*

*Your body responses are
mapped into Holy Mind perfectly.*

Reflect a little on this now. Muse about it!

What an amazing trick of deception and perception.

Eating good food.

Same, marvel at the absolute magnificence and miracle of Incarnation in this virtual experience.

Staying warm in the winter.

Same, use this to remember the warmth of your Loving Holy Family.

Comfort is also naturally built in from ancient memory.

Going for a swim in the deep ocean.

Same, with an addition of feeling Deep Freedom. The Holy Mind is as deep as the ocean.

> *"You are now on Earth to experience*
> *Holiness Inside Freedom,*
> *without external interference*
>
> *or manipulation at any level".*

You may be locked up physically at some point, but they cannot lock up your mind, remember this.

Even inside chains and deprivation, your Holy Peace of Mind and Holy Joy can shine out, showing Holy Self Love.

> *All these Holy things are natural and normal,*
> *being built in from the beginning*
> *as an ancient memory*
> *and holding these up for others to view*
> *reflects Holiness in Self Love.*
>
> *Bushel Basket message again.*

Going to visit a friend that you really love being around, just for the comfort and the dreamy time and fun.

Any activity that is natural and almost automatic that invokes Peace or Joy is reflecting Holiness in Self Love.

*Not letting your left hand know
what your right hand is doing in the way of giving,
is reflecting Holiness in Self Love.*

Out of Holy Abundance it will flow.

There are no ulterior motives, just Holiness and Purity flowing. Notice these things and smile and appreciate.

Ego is tied to scarcity
with many controls and controllers.

Ego thoughts are making that scarcity feeling.

Holiness is inside this somewhere waiting to pop out.}

And so, we are now starting to enter into more simplicity again.

*"You do not have to prove
to yourself or others you are spiritual
by some belief, thought, activity or speech
or look or book."*

You are spiritual and so are all the others. Smile at them if they are not aware of this.

Wave "A Hello".

"Hello, Holy Ones, I see you"!

This is an act of Holiness in Self Love. (You have

withdrawn judgement and replaced it with the Holy Blessing.)

> *Doing yoga, or chanting or being a vegetarian*
> *or thinking you are woke in some way*
> *or a Christian or a Buddhist*
> *or a scholar is not spiritual,*
> *it is just a thing, a belief thing,*
> *an ego mental activity thing,*
> *an ego thought thing,*
> *An ego human duality thing,*
>
> *All ego idea things.*

The spiritual part (Holy Child) is the living in the framework and flow of Holy Karma, displaying Joy and Peace even while doing any manual labour or the programming or the calculus or the folding up of limbs and the breath on the mat.

Many that practise these ego modality ideas above are in a Holy Space much of the time. They just haven't worked out yet, it is not the modality.

> *It will never be those belief things*
> *that are of importance in your life,*
> *it will only be allowing the flow of*
> *Holy Karma inside Holy Self Love.*
> *See this clearly, I am holy not because*
> *of the Yoga or any other modality at all,*
> *it is because I was birthed from Holiness*
> *and that is enough.*

Got that? Say that! Keep That!

Even inside all of those belief structures, you can be touching Holiness in Self Love moment by moment, all day.

Moving along into this mental state of Holy Normality is reflecting Holiness in Self Love.

You are becoming as you really are, in simplicity, in Holiness, Flowing Holy Karma.

I release the need to prove my spirituality; this is reflecting Holiness in Self Love. There is cause in that need, find it.

I release the need to feel special; this is reflecting Holiness in Self Love. There is cause in that also, find it.

The need in all of these ego-based deceptions is a hidden cause. Find it and release it as ego cause and unneeded resistant energy to Holiness. You are Holy already.

I treasure my new simplicity of thought as an act of Holiness in Self Love.

I decide now I am complete; I was birthed this way; this is reflecting Holiness in Self Love.

I desire to feel Holiness always, like when I drink my health shake each morning. Ha.

It cannot be any other way.

And you possibly thought Holy Karma would only be some sort of ecstasy.

Note that these simple things above are ecstasy when running in Holy Karma.

And you know this and have experienced it many times.

When living in ego-distorted automatic mentality, these types of awareness moments are often lost.

Hold on to the moments and then release the moment with Holy Gratitude.

Divinity must exist in you to appreciate all of this as a Natural Holy Response.

Life here or there, this domain or that one over there, is always like this when running in Holy Karma. Pure natural, normal.

> *Many people who say they have passed through the veil of so-called body death, and see the light at the end of the tunnel and then come back to body life again by reconnecting to body DNA creation, almost always say it was "Bliss"*

on the other side (singularity)
where they went to
and they did not want to come back.

The guy with the clipboard said,
"You are too early, there is more for you yet,
back you go",
Oh no that trapdoor thing again!

Bring that Bliss into Virtuality Creations by allowing Holy Karma to Flow Love through you continually, untouched but admired and appreciate with a big breath out in Holiness in Self Love.

Pretend you have just arrived on Earth; however, this time you know who you really are. Imagine how you would live, yes imagine, until it becomes true for you. Holy Spirit flowing in Holy Karma activity.

Love to all the Holy Deciders

Love to you all from Shamaré

The Protector
The Door Keeper
The Gatekeeper
The Guardian of the Holy Karma Arising Now

8.
Holy Karma > Holiness in Clarity

Holiness in Clarity comes as "The mist of ego misidentification, that is, body-self DNA deception, is slowly cleared and is lifted off from the Holy Mind, by the Holy Spirit.

> Holy Spirit is the "Great Soother of all Minds, those that allow it, even unknowingly".
> How have you ever been healed of anything?

This Holiness in Clarity is another one of early awareness changes or additions that leads a misidentified mind back to Holy Karma, the required Gethsemane state.

> This Awareness is a return to True Normalcy, the Actual Natural, that is "Identifying as Spirit".

Yes, your true family, Divinity itself.

Sanity returning with the arrival of Holiness in Clarity.

Not by learning anything new but by allowing and surrendering to Holy Spirit.

Not by invoking but by trusting.

Not by good works but by embracing the flow of Holy Karma once again.

Holy Spirit Self is the only thing that truly exists.

The Holy Self are all the Holy Children as One.

> "The Father and I are one".
> Jeshua's thoughts on it.
>
> Another thought for you.
>
> Love your neighbour as yourself!
>
> They are you also. That changes the meaning!

Yes, nothing else really exists except the Holy Natural. No work required, no learning, just surrendered.

Holiness in Clarity, for some, comes instantly, in one giant hit or flash.

For others it is many lifetimes of slowly developing enough Holy Self Love to finally allow the Holiness in Clarity to bloom.

A long gestation of many endeavours, wrong roads taken and getting lost many times along the way.

For those that have an instant experience, it is very rare, it requires a full surrender without any conditions that might get in the way. If you can let go of everything in a flash and surrender, it will happen.

For the many, it is a series of many small steps, often imperceivable, but nevertheless, still steps.

"Many are inside the small steps unknowingly at this time." Tiptoeing along.

Holiness in Clarity is a part of the bigger Holy Jigsaw.

Yes, another Jigsaw Piece.

Holiness in Clarity could be considered one of the Corner Pieces of the Puzzle.

Holy Self Love is at the top right side, Holiness in Clarity on the top left side.

Picture that layout, put them in place now. You know you want to. Just do it and sigh.

Say out loud, "It is taking shape! I am good at puzzles!"

Now, hunt through all the pieces available to you and find the pieces around that left top corner piece and you have extended imagination and add more structural possibilities.

Once your Awareness starts to open with Holiness

in Clarity, the other pieces will start to show themselves and they fit easily together and an outline of Holy Karma will start to take shape in front of you mentally and flow into your feelings and imagination, with more possibilities.

When the pieces are all in place and there is no more mind work going on, you can allow the seeing of the complete picture and it is done, not by effort.

The last step is made by Holy Divinity, so get out of the way and allow it to come to you.

Imagine this, imagine this more, consider deeply the imagination of Holy Karma. See it, a new Holy World arising because of it.

Say to yourself,
"I have imagined all of this,
now in Holiness in Clarity,
I am seeing the actuality flowing in front of me.
Imagine everyone doing this "imagining",

It will happen"! Big days are ahead.

Holiness in Clarity comes as you start to recognise the shapes and colours of Holy Karma in imagination, allowing you to find the pieces rapidly.

Imagination is only ever born from actuality; you do know this already and so it is now being reborn from old memory by you and for you.

Occasionally you will find you get stuck and the picture doesn't seem to want to finish.

But allow Holiness in Clarity with Holy Knowledge to come through that blocking ego noise, Holiness in Clarity will show the pieces in the puzzle that seemed so hard to find and match. Sink into this experience. Call out loud for some help.

*This stalled state will often happen when
you are running some sort of
projection judgement issue
with someone who you consider has wronged you
or affecting you and then everything grinds to a halt.*

Until this is let go and healing is done.

See them Holy Only also.

Healing as Holiness in Clarity allows you to develop a change in viewpoint for others around you, with the realisation of this one statement being true for you also.

This statement is true at the most basic level. Say:

*"No one has ever really done a single thing to me,
as all the reactivity is birthed directly in my own Mind."*

And with the birth of this Holy Realisation comes a cosmic shift in viewpoint, from projection out at others, to introspection of Self/self and forgiveness for the projections and the misperceptions that drove them.

Holiness in Clarity arising. Holy Karma showing itself more brightly each day.

> "I now understand the 'Mirror Story'.
> All is mirroring to me only myself at all times".

Thank you, Holiness in Clarity.

> Judgements of others is let go
> and a brighter Holy Clarity arises,
> with a settling down of the Holy Mind at last,
> allowing the Holy Observations
> of the workings of your own Holy Mind.

> This new awareness of your own unawareness
> now becomes the theme of the new Holy Karma Life.

This is a very potent moment when this arrives. It is only a choice away.

> The world is innocent
> in a flash of Holiness in Clarity.
> Wow.

> All is ego illusion and ego projection from me.

Additional to this introspection of self is an arising Awareness in Holiness in Clarity on the human world and your part in it.

"Thoughts on your human family, culture, beliefs, status

and what it is all for and about."

Also, Holiness in Clarity fills in all the unanswered questions about Mother Earth and with what the ego world propaganda says, it will just sink away as nothing of value.

> *"Not of the world but in it,*
> *as observer only now,*
>
> *in Holiness in Clarity."*

This is a slight addition to Jeshua's words. Are we able to share the copyright?

The grand politics of nothing, the superfluous intellect, the trapping religions, the dividing cultural beliefs and much more.

Look carefully at the distorting "cultures of honour". Discard this as a mental poison.

All that anxiety, worry and concern is healed as Holiness in Clarity arises.

Going forward, there is a progression to a deeper Holiness in Clarity, as it is Holy Karma that is directing you now.

Let's examine the possible mechanisms for this.

> *And so, you have realised*
> *the thing you disliked the most about*

one of your parents, brothers or sisters or friends, is actually dwelling deep inside you, as a monster in the dark.

Could I forgive myself if I was like them?!

That's a big one, Holiness in Clarity.

Many will say you are mad to think this way; they are stuck in ego retribution.

Let them go, smile and move into healing Holy Realisations. Let the realisations flow into your awareness for healing. They will come in the night often; don't miss the message.

It may also be time to crawl into your mental basement and rummage around and find it all, maybe a bit spooky down there but it will surely bring greater Holiness in Clarity as the baggage of projected judgements are thrown out as trash.

Once you have done this, there will be repeat and repeat with many family members until the new arising energy is only Holy Compassion and Holy Love for them all, with Holy Gratitude.

Most importantly also, you're releasing them from your power of judgement will allow them an easier road to wander down in their own awakening travels that they may unknowingly be involved at this point. And they are!

All are going to do this walk and you do know now how it is a very interesting experience of finding yourself always being in the way of yourself. Make it easier for them to do the walk; release the judgement.

Holiness in Clarity now shines the light on Holy Love Flowing to All (The Holy Cause) and Holy Karma now asks of you, as Holy Effect, to heal yourself and drop judgment projection.

This is another lifting of the Bushel Basket moment, step into it well.

The Jigsaw is filling in. All those red pieces now click together easily.

My bully brother is actually my saviour. All those years of strife with him, now show clearly, I was resisting healing and causing great suffering for myself, as the misperceived victim. He held his role well, maybe unknowingly.

My mother's inability to show compassion to her children,
now shines the light on my releasing the need to hold her as guilty and to take the big hint

and be compassionate to her and all others.

How does that work?

Because this can be a big one to let go of.

Holiness in Clarity allows you to see that your mother was ego misperceiving also, unaware and not in Holiness in Clarity but did her best inside those ego limitations because of Love flowing as mother/nurturer. (A lot or a little.) You chose your mother for this reason and more. She taught you well.

It doesn't matter how much flowed, she did flow love sometimes but was unable to shed enough mental rubbish due to lack of Holy Self Love, so Holiness in Clarity never arose as an option. It was always a struggle for her. However, at some point, she, as will all, have to allow healing to come. You may very well be the one to open this possibility by pulling judgement off her and free her to open more.

Reapply the above to a father if required. (Anyone!)

My so-called friends at school who were bullying me for so long, now I can see they were ego hurting also and were only projecting all of their ego hurt at me.

I am the beneficiary of their projections,
I can see my sovereignty is
unaffected by all of this now
and my Holiness in Clarity

> *allows me to now say to them,*
> *"Come let us all heal together"*
> *whether out loud to them*
> *or in private to Holy Self.*

> *"I now release the world, I release the goings on,*
> *the noise, the rights and wrongs,*
> *the proofs and the provers, the cancellers and the cancelled.*

> *They can sort all of that out now with the Holy Spirit, not me.*

Holy Karma has called, Holiness in Clarity has arisen and I see into the distance (imagination again) a full birth of Holy Karma coming, as a new Heaven and new Earth.

Keep this imagination until the reality, a new Heaven and new Earth, with healed Holy Ego, the dropping of the misperception of body DNA ego, and the arising of Real Divine Ego, Holy Karma.

A New Heaven and New Earth, the dwelling place for the many in Holy Karma.

The Holy Minds that are aware they are inside Reality already with true perception are wrapped in Holy Divinity and are now back inside the True Holy Family Domain once again, knowing they never left, only in dreams.

Holiness in Clarity will reveal knowings about the arising New Earth. Miraculous expanded Holy Knowings.

In the New Earth, the human DNA body continues and now resides for you, for the purpose of your Holy Mind to play inside of it and allow out Holy Karma effect to bring forth Holy Action with Holy Outcomes.

Finally experiencing Divinity through Holy Karma, inside the New Earth creation but not really, perceiving all of this only and always in the One Mind inside Reality or Divinity.

And in that day of the arising New Heaven and a New Earth,
Holy Spirit acting in all present, via Holy Karma,
brings forth a shower of Holiness in Clarity
unseen on this planet for a long time.
New colours, new freshness, new beauty, new appreciation,
new expansive freedom, now only Holy Love flowing.

Now all present have this Holy Awareness

"That only Holy Love is Real".

No ego government required, no ego laws to bind the mind up. Divine Holy Purpose flows direct from the Holy Universal Divine Body to all via the activating energy of the Holy Spirit as Holy Love.

Peace at Last. Peace at Last. (He will be happy to see it.)

Blessed are the Holy Ones that will see this dawn, for they will see God (in themselves and others).

Blessed are the Holy Ones that have chosen Holy Right-ness, for they will dwell in Holy Karma.

Blessed are the meek that have sought Holy Peace, for they will live in this Holy Peace for ever.

Love to all those in Holiness in Clarity.

Love to you all from Shamaré

The Protector
The Door Keeper
The Gatekeeper
The Guardian of the Holy Karma Arising Now

9.
Holy Karma > Holiness in Joy

Joy is one of the primary mental states that arise for any entity living in the flow of Holy Karma anywhere. Here, there or over there. Same energy.

Actually, there is only Reality to live in and it is multidimensional and infinite.

> *Joy does not require any prerequisites*
> *to arise in any entity.*
> *Whether here or there,*
> *that is the Third Dimension*
> *or the Ninth Dimension (Ninth Heaven),*
> *Joy flows out as the*
> *Natural Surrendered Holy Mental State*
>
> *Without effort or thought.*

Notice the word entity is used, but we can substitute soul if we like. A soul is an entity in individuated experience.

An entity in Joy is always in the Flow of Holy Karma, and it arises and stays permanently as one of the natural divine mental states and gifts.

An entity not in the flow of Holy Karma, that is, one choosing wrong-mindedness, will fluctuate their mental state even right into the mental states of despair and self-loathing in some cases.

In other words, Joy only truly arises and is embedded when Holy Karma is flowing.

Entities in Joy do not apply any wrong-mindedness trans-muting mental energy to this flow of Divine Holy Love.

They leave Love Energy in its Pure, Holy or in its Divine Wholeness. Untouched by thought or need!

What makes this possible is a mental state of surrendering back to the simplicity of singularity, back to original Holy Purpose and what arises immediately is the original Holy Mental State that all were birthed with.

The Original Holy "you" is now re-embedding their Holy Purpose, and this lifts an entity out of ego expression.

The decision may look like this one.
These words of old are a quite appropriate decision now:

"Not my will be done but thine be done."

That is the full surrender from ego misperception back to the simplicity and singularity in Holiness.

Even when body dying on a cross, in DNA body pain, the master teacher of Holy Karma was able to extend compassion while maintaining Holy Peace by allowing Joy to flow.

*For those that orchestrated the day's events,
he said, "Father forgive them
for they do not know what they do."*

*They were only killing a body, a creation,
not the entity, the I am.*

No judgement or bitterness or fear, just Holy Joy flowing. Just a change in where you hang out really.

The combination of the two words, Holy and Joy, is not actually required.

Only Joy really needs to be said as Joy is only ever a Holy Mental state and not available to ego mentality.

And so, you can see the mental state of Joy can survive and flow out in even the most trying of circumstance because of Holy Knowing.

This is very different from happiness.

Happiness is an ego mental state where prerequisites are to be meet.

"I am not happy today because…!"

"I am unhappy today because…!"

Ego karma mentality flows happiness on expectation or loss of expectation.

The Holy Surrender solidly locks in Joy and Peace of mind.

You will know you are there when all remains still in the mind, even during what the ego would regard as trying times.

Love to all the Surrenders and those at Holy Peace and in Holiness in Joy.

Love to you all from Shamaré

The Protector
The Door Keeper
The Gatekeeper
The Guardian of the Holy Karma Arising Now

10.
Holy Karma > Holiness in Peace of Mind

After millennia of ego mental struggle,
living inside illusions of dualities,
it is time at last for the Arising of Peace of Mind
for the participating souls
that volunteered for the grand experiment
of being and believing
they are separated from Divine Holy Source.

Holiness in Peace of Mind.

In this duality ego world experience, we have attempted to create virtual substitutes for all the things in Home Reality that we were birthed into.

Most of all the family and with it many cultures that have meaning, belief systems that attempt to bring stability and peace of mind, even justice systems to keep good in the forefront and evil at the back. A pseudo-conditional peace.

We have attempted to create ego mimics of our Real Selves. Building and making, learning and exploring our own creation, as if we didn't know anything about it. Ha.

*The time is upon us in every incarnation,
at any moment to dump it all
and move into Holy Karma with full realisation of*

*who we really are and what and why
we are in the virtuality.*

At that very moment for all and any, Holy Peace of Mind arises, the prodigal son and daughter return home to a grand home welcoming and it is done. Except maybe for the chatter afterwards.

Gold stars are handed out to all, and a party runs for some time.

*How else could Holy Peace of Mind arise?
There is no other way; we have tried them all.*

That is the purpose of the experiment

to become fully realised that
*"**Only Love is Real**".*

Even a hobby of collecting stamps is fraught with moments of desperation when the discovery is made that the most valuable one is a forgery. Ha.

Yes, the return to full original Holy Family is the only way to Holy Peace of Mind with the realisation "That **Only Love is Real**" and it has been sitting there waiting to be rediscovered by all the little lost souls.

So, my dear, dear friends, waste not another moment

on misperceptions, misunderstanding, ego projection but return home mentally to Holy Divine Singularity,

your Holy Family, your Birth right True Spirit DNA.

The multi-dimensional helix of Divine Holy Energy that you are.

Your Holiness only ever arises when Holy Peace of Mind envelops your Holy Entity.

Love to all those allowing Holy Peace of Mind to flow through them once again.

Love to you all from Shamaré

The Protector
The Door Keeper
The Gatekeeper
The Guardian of the Holy Karma Arising Now

11.
Holy Karma > Holiness in Communication

And what would you communicate in the flow of Holy Karma? Holiness.

> *The primary driving force*
> *behind all Holy Communication*
> *or Holy Communion is that*
> "**Only Holy Love is Real**".

> *Holiness in Singularity, with focus.*

Holy Love can be abbreviated to just Love, as Love doesn't exist outside Holiness. There are mimics or attempts to simulate Holy Love in ego incarnation.

"Anything else other than the mental state of Love is a cry for help and healing" – Jeshua.

This dispels the notion of normality inside the flow of ego mind. Impossible!

Yes, many would have you conform your statements so as to normalise ego insanity.

> *They will surely say to you,*
> *"Isn't this information good and correct!?"*

"Doesn't this help with the human mental state?"

You are now free to communicate from Holy Mind and this is always driven by Holy Spirit directing the thoughts, if you pay attention.

*Communicate only this,
"The Good, the Holy and the Beautiful".*

Jeshua again.

You may surprise yourself and others when you waggle the tongue now and blow out noisy air.

Well done, it will make all the difference communicating and speaking from Holiness.

Judgement, Fear and Guilt may not enter the Holy Communication words any further.

*Some of you will speak incredibly boldly
and create quite a stir*

in the ego world with your Holy Communication.

Even some of the old ego world philosophies and religions will have to step back and say this communication is based on information from Divine Source and it is beautiful to hear.

*When addressing groups now
use the time in the introduction
to call all present as the*

> *"Holy Children" arising from the*
> *One Grand Holy Intelligence of Consciousness.*

They may gasp, keep doing it until the denial is put to rest.

> *And with that short note go forth*
> *and Communicate in Holiness using simple direct words*
> *to the Holy Children still asleep in ego mind.*

Love to all those Communicating in Holiness once again.

For those communicating with words living in Holy Karma, words can be less efficient than a direct communication mind to mind, with this type of transmission missing out the fact that words are symbols of symbols, twice removed from Reality. A little fluffy sometimes.

It is often better to feel the words, rather than interpret the words for their meaning.

This means communication will take on a method of evoke response rather than just teaching information.

Do not forget the student (Spirit Entity) with the DNA Body standing in front of your DNA Body is Holy and knows all of this information already, as they are Holy Family also.

*The trick in Holy Communication
with the ego student is to
evoking feelings of remembrance
of forgotten Holy Family
and their own Holiness.*

*You are the light of the world.
Don't hide your Holiness under a bushel basket,*

Let it shine before all people.

The Teacher for God, you, is the same as the student, for as you speak you remind and teach yourself also. Equality for both listener and communicator.

Communication is also available in body world actions.

Love to you all as you communicate in Holiness.

Love to you all from Shamaré

The Protector
The Door Keeper
The Gatekeeper
The Guardian of the Holy Karma Arising Now

12.
Holy Karma > Holiness in Being

Being is the mental "Projection of Holy Self (the I Am – Holy Entity) into a domain that allows for a duality virtuality".

This mental projection in this case is into a domain of ego mental deception, with dualities because that is the project we have created and designed for ourselves, to have the experience inside of.

How well will you maintain your Holiness,
while in this Duality Domain,
if you are aware and know your singularity nature?

What you mentally project out at any time
is always "Your Desire".

Therefore incarnating is "Being" or "being", Holy or ego.

In a Holy Mind, running inside Holy Karma the "Projection is always Singularity and therefore Holy, expressing as Joy, Peace of Mind and Love Flowing unhindered, unaltered", with great Holy Self Love.

In ego mind, running inside
a deceptive ego mental framework,

> *the "mental projection is always in duality*
> *and therefore with distortion of Holiness*
> *and the flow of Holy Love gets transmuted into*
> *arising fears, guilts and projected judgements*
> *about many things".*

The game plan behind this type of Incarnation (the knowing of flesh) is to finally return to the Holy Mental State of only "experiencing mental projection as a Holy Being, in Singularity again, recovered, seeing only Holiness and Singularity always. Can this be achieved?

This experience is exactly determined by how you are mentally projecting, either Being or being.

> *With the Arising of Holy Awareness,*
> *that is, you know now you are fundamentally*
> *a Spirit and also Holy,*
> *then Holy Karma is the experience that is Arising.*
> *This is Being, a Holy Being,*
>
> *even using a DNA body for the Holy Projection*
> *experience.*

This Arising Holy Karma is driven by desires and intentions of Holy Self Love and Holy Choices being made, with the assistance always of the ever-present Holy Spirit, the grand orchestrator for those in Holy Alliance, Holy Allowance, Holy Trust and Holy Embrace of all things Divine, in Singularity.

Holiness will always arise naturally for you, in mental surrender, it cannot be any other way.

It is just the fundamental natural Holy State arising, inside the state of Reality.

Holy Karma is the treasure that flows from inside this Holy Surrender.

And with that simple precise opening, you are safe to explore Being in Holiness even with a DNA body.

There is more yet to discuss on "Being" in further chapters.

Suffice to say, there is a very large clue in the identification tag assigned to the Human Incarnation.

This Tag is: "Human Being"

Or

"I Am – Being Human".
The "I Am" is the Holy Self.

The "Being Human" is the DNA Vehicle Robot for virtual experience.

So Being Human is projecting Holy Self (the "I Am") into the matrix of energy called a human body to dwell in an energy of duality for a while to experience cause and effects in the mind from Dualities.

This is the original purpose for the creation long ago, for the experience and for the Being or the being.

Remember the original Question that has started the whole process of experience?

> What would it be like to live in a world
> where "Only Love is Not Real"?

> So, the duality experience it seems must be had
> and then because of your Holiness,
> awareness naturally arises
> to set you free from the ego entanglement of it all.

> How goes the disentanglement?

If you weren't incarnating as a Human Being, you may very well be incarnating into another experience as that Being or being.

Maybe Star Child Being or similar. Imagine this!

And if you withdraw from the entanglement of Incarnating in Duality and arrive home disentangled, your status will be Spirit Entity (I Am) again, swirling in the one light with all the other Light Entities that also are "I Ams", in individuation. Not a Being or being any further.

*And so, you can see Being or being
can be magnificent or dreadful,
it is entirely up to you to
"Decide how to Be or be".
If it is dreadful or difficult,
it is being, not Being (ego being).*

*To Be or Not to Be,
this is the question.*

And your answer is: you have to decide to Be (or be).

And so here you are (supposedly), (pretending), (full embodied) playing as being human, experiencing Duality in some level of insanity.

And via Holy Awareness Arising due to developing Holy Self Love, Holy Decisions, Holy Spirit, you can

*"Be"
Love itself again in Singularity.
Living in the Christ Sane Mind.
In Spirit Home and in Reality.*

or

*"be"
Love and Hate in Duality.
Living in an insane ego illusional world
with a mind in fear, guilt and judgement.*

Possibly with a DNA Body that is having difficulty also.

Choose the first one, to Be.

Say "I chose the Holy Mind of Christ; the ego mind is just causing all sorts of mental and emotional issues".

Do not waste another moment in the second one, that is, being. Choose Holiness now, it is your true and natural State.

And with that we will leave you to Be or be as you decide and choose.

Being as Human or being as Human

or

maybe Being or being as something else.

Somewhere?

How about a dog? They get treats and tummy scratches regularly.

All are creations and mental projections and not Reality Holy Home.

> The "I Am" remains untouched, unchanged and is always Holy.

Love to all those playing as Beings or beings.

Love to you all from Shamaré

The Protector
The Door Keeper
The Gatekeeper
The Guardian of the Holy Karma Arising Now

13.
Holy Karma > Holiness in Actions

On entering Holy Karma energy, it will become obvious very quickly that most Holy Action is no longer planned by you directly, but it will flow to you via Holy Spirit activation. You will be moved to Holiness in Action.

Day to day what will arise for you is your purpose naturally without thought.

> *Not every day will there be*
> *something of great importance*
> *to go and participate in some way.*
> *In fact each morning can be started*
> *with a quiet internal Holy Question.*

"What would be my Holy Action today?"

And if nothing comes up into the mind, do as you please for the day, go fishing or sleep under a tree, plants some seeds, weed the garden, say hello to some friends.

If communication from Holy Spirit does arise for

you, move easily into that Holy Moment, with direction and allowing it to unfold naturally for you.

It is not your Intellectual function to decide all of this, it will arise in your Holy Mind for you from deep down in the multi-dimensional layers of Holy Self.

You are not a Holy Slave,
you are a Holy Entity
that is now moving back
into your pure Holy Role of
receiving direction and creating Holy Action.
And finally my dear friends,
if you are in this state of Holy Action,
you are a Holy Ascended Master yourself.

Your purpose is now before you in a multitude of ways.

However, it is not with a personal goal
or a thought that you proceed.
Holy Action is the merging together of Holy Spirit
with your Holy Individuated Spirit
to create Holy Outcomes
or to move things along in some way
for some Holy purpose.

Trust this always.

The Holy Outcomes are not to be counted or documented in any way but just allowed to come into Being and then move on to the next identified moment or purpose using Holy Karma.

Cause and effect. You are Holy Effect at this point.

It is not up to you to decide the outcome or force it to happen.

Sometimes what looked like a failed outcome is actually what is required at this moment for that one.

Allowance flows from a peaceful mind with only Holy Joy.

Never expectations.

*The Holy Outcome is not up to you,
other than you allow yourself to be moved to Holy Action
and speak and be involved in the action
that is being aroused at that Holy Moment.*

These will come frequently and without effort

As allowance is perfected in surrender.

And so there you are, incarnated but co-creating with the invisible, seemingly from a body.

That is a joke of course.

Always, Holy Action arises in Holy Mind.

En-joy this, relish it, bathe yourself in it.

*Your purpose is clear now,
creating more and more of the same,*

endlessly and without effort.
physical manifesting may occur at any point,
accept this as a Holy Function to complete some action.
Move silently through all of this

and grow in Holy Appreciation of your now clear
Holy Path Arising.

And with that short, short directed summary, move into Holy Action often.

Love to all those allowing Holy Action to flow through them.

Love to you all from Shamaré

The Protector
The Door Keeper
The Gatekeeper
The Guardian of the Holy Karma Arising Now

14.
Holy Karma > Holiness in Serving

It may occur via internal communication through the one mind that you are being asked to serve in some capacity.

Serving is often a passive or less active involvement in assistance of another. This is not something to fuss about. It is just a simple step in and out process, where needed.

Some examples of this Holiness in Serving can be:

This is similar to Holy Action
For a short moment,
hold open a spiritual transformation opportunity
for another to move into Holiness.

Most Holy Service is longer term.

For a longer moment,
hold the role supporting many, as Teacher or Principal.

The Teacher role will be to support others who are in misperception of true Holy Self, although they are now ready to free themselves but may have some old fears holding the process back. A Teacher may give confidence.

And then again, you may be asked to serve by retiring into the wilderness to sit in clarity for a lengthy time.

Did you know you can replicate this wilderness mental state idea in the day to day, even while working?

Just open yourself to serve anywhere and anytime and then carry on as normal, serving away, as singularity helps dissolve away resistance in the mind matrix of others.

Normal is staying aware of what is flowing for you in background mind.

Holiness in Serving is always with openness and willingness as what is being undertaken

is not for gain or status but being of help continually!

Serving with friends or family can be just smiling and allowing, not interfering and trying to fix things but allowing of the long term to heal itself. The service is to stay out of judgement and projection.

Serving to bring Heaven to Earth.

Trust the moments of serving.

*Say I am open to serve now!
Co-creating and helping transform duality
to heaven on earth in singularity is Holy serving.
More than likely this will be the mode
for many until the transmutation is complete.*

*You are going to see miraculous days ahead,
even moment by moment.*

As you move deeper into your Holiness, your Holy Serving will become part of the fabric of the Universe.

Unknowingly now, you are involved in this, even if it is fleeting and sporadic at present.

*This Mental Activity will progressively steady out
and your function as Holy Server will solidify
with the progressive allowance of*

Additional Holy Karma flow.

You are on your way to be of great service to the Holy ones who are unaware as yet.

Love to all those allowing Holy Service to flow through them.

Love to you all from Shamaré

The Protector
The Door Keeper

The Gatekeeper
The Guardian of the Holy Karma Arising Now

15.
Holy Karma > Holiness in Transparency

*With the arising of Holy Karma
comes the understanding
that privacy and secrets are a thing of the past.
There is only One Holy Mind shared by the Holy Family.*

*Families do not have secrets if they are Holy
(that is, when all are Whole, Aware
and Conscious in a Holy Way).*

*So, living inside Holiness with Transparency
is the accepted state.*

It is just how it is naturally.

If you feel you can have secrecy and privacy inside the flow of Holy Karma, there is an immediate exit from the flow as it is an impossibility. Bring out the secrets and dump them.

*In other words,
Holy Transparency is not a requirement or a rule.
It is not even a thought.*

It is just how it is naturally.

You mean I have to undress my beliefs and thoughts publicly?

Well, inside Holy Karma there are no strong beliefs, it is how it is, solid and permanent and to ask for privacy with a belief is an absurd mental construct.

You could fabricate the idea into a virtualisation like the earth, world, humans live inside and experience it.

Oh, I forgot, that is what is being done right now. Ha.

So, you can see Transparency will just arise as normal inside Holy Karma.
Now imagine living in a world where all is open and exposed and discussed without judgement.
Yes, Heaven on Earth Arising.
No fear limiting,
No guilt pangs,

with
No personal judgement.

No wonder there will be Peace on earth and great Joy beyond ego understanding.

Moving on. It is getting easier.

Singularity is the key.
"Only Love is Real."

How could Privacy fit into that way of living?

Love to all those Transforming with Holy Transparency.

Love to you all from Shamaré

The Protector
The Door Keeper
The Gatekeeper
The Guardian of the Holy Karma Arising Now

16.
Holy Karma > Holiness in Transformation

Stepping into Holy Karma is as a Holy Rebirth.

What does this Holy Rebirth mean?

Re-Birth means you have already been birthed but now you are doing it again!

Wow! How?

> It is almost like a resurrection,
> coming back to life again,
> as a new entity
> with many mental changes.

How this happens must be a Holy Transformation.

If this is the case, then Holiness is Arising, by stepping into the energy of Holy Karma.

What does this Transformation mean?

To transform is to change from one form to another form.

So now not only have you rebirthed but you have changed Form!

What have you become with all of this Transforming?

You were originally Birthed as Holy Child arising from Holy Source as part of Divinity.

With Rebirth and Transformation, you arise as this Holy type again with expanded experience and awareness.

> The Rebirth is metaphorical
> because you were never lost as Holy Child,
>
> only a sleep dreaming that you weren't a Holy Child.

The Holy Transform is again metaphorical and it is only happening in Holy Mind.

From being to Being.

From ego karma to Holy Karma.

From insanity to Holy Sanity again.

From lost to found (this is only true in personal awareness).

> I was lost to myself, asleep dreaming
> I was a victim separated from Holy Self and Holy Source.
> I have found My Holy Self again,

> *it was always there waiting for me*
> *to drop the dream slumber.*

Holiness in Transformation is a miracle to outside observers. What will they all say?

They ask how this is possible, as we are stuck and making no progress! As if in Hell! Give us a drop of Holy water please.

> *Holy Transformation is the work*
> *between a willing Holy Mind*
>
> *and the Holy Spirit, the great Transformer.*

And there you have it once again in simplicity.

Have you noticed by now, you know all of this stuff. It is the only natural outcome possible. Simplicity itself.

We could stop here and leave it to your imagination for the rest of the book. Quite possible.

However, I have been told to complete and you will just have to follow along. You can dream up your own extensions for the book. If they follow the Singularity of **"Only Love is Real"**, you are in the game truly.

Holy Karma providing energy to do the Holy Transform to full Holy Awareness.

I am but Spirit, a Holy Child,

loved forever and alive forever.

Love to all those Arising with Holy Transformation.

Love to you all from Shamaré

The Protector
The Door Keeper
The Gatekeeper
The Guardian of the Holy Karma Arising Now

17.
Holy Karma > Holiness in Trans-Mutation

*Transmutation of the ego duality mind
back to Holy Singularity Mind
is the game in this domain.
The reversing of the mutations in ego mind
backwards to purity of mind.*

*The changing of one type of nature
to another type of nature.
(Or back to natural or original or birthed nature).*

Holiness Arising.

From Type insane to Type Holy.

Type Misidentified mind to Type True-Identified Mind.

Misunderstandings in an ego mind to Holy Knowing in a Holy Mind.

The end of ego projection with judgement to the allowing of Holy Karma flow with Grace.

The converting of ego lead to Holy Gold.

All of these ideas are to help you understand how Transmutation is going to happen, a mini miracle.

How to end those ego judgements?

That is the projection out at and to others of their faults; you do know that the same faults are in yourself!

How to end the Hate and Anger?

That is the projection out to others of your own ego self-loathing you know and feel about yourself.

How to end distorting the Holy Energy of Divine Love into another form that creates dualities?

That is the projection out to others that you are lost and forgotten somehow and now totally separated from Holy Source living in a created DNA body somewhere.

And the list goes on.

*What or Whom could possibly be that powerful
that these mental projections could all end
and Holy Peace reigns again,
inside the framework of Holy Joy?*

*And the answer is:
My dear friends, it is "You".
Let me further introduce your ego self
to your True Holy Self.*

Always and forever, all the beliefs and resulting ego projections are all your own creations.

All the writhing and self-loathing is only the ego self, trying to scare ego self. You do that well.

This all leads to a feeling and mental attitude of disempowerment and resulting victimhood, being stuck at some level, conscious or unconscious.

Or

You are just making yourself feel stuck, emotionally, mentally and being as a frail "Human Being".

> *Do not forget that Holy Love is the only true energy and you are bathed in it moment by moment.*
>
> *Divine Love flows to you and through you, not from a source apart from you*
>
> *but from a source in the very depth of you.*

That is where the Holy Love in Singularity comes from, "You" as part of Divinity.

This Holy Energy is the thing that you distort inside your great freedom and with your great power into projections of dualities in all forms. "You do it all!" You are very good at scaring yourself.

And so once again, you are the one that needs to

take responsibility for ego insane mental projection and the ego noise and nip it in the bud.

In doing this nipping, it ceases to grow and instead it withers away forever. It will not flower now.

And you do the "nipping" often day to day, moment by moment unconsciously, sometimes you see it but ignore the power flowing.

It is a Holy Decision: I nip!

Hence all the words in the book, all the symbols to invoke recognition, emotion, desire, intention and allowance until you finally step into the Holy Surrender, that is become and allowing Holy Karma itself.

In the surrender, all Holiness starts naturally flowing again for you.

The Transmutation of mind back to Holiness.

Every single thing that is not Holy in your mind,
can be undone by you and you alone,
as it is only your creation.

And you can thank the Holy Heavens for this,
because if this existence as "Human Being"
was Reality and not creation,

you would be powerless to change even a single piece of it.

So, knowing this might enliven you to step into the ownership of all your creations and drop them as unholy.

They are masking and keeping you from Holy Singularity Itself, that is residing in Holy Karma.

Ego creations can only exist
off ego-projected energy that feeds them.
Yes, you are feeding your own
creations, beliefs, viewpoints,
misperception, misunderstandings
with mutated Holy Love.

It is as simple as deciding
to stop mutating your Love Flow

and allowing Holiness to take effect
and flow once again.

When you step out of the picture as ego self, and step into another picture as Holy Karma, Holy Love itself, in Holiness, Holy Love flows again untouched.

You could say that if you get out of the way mentally, Holy Transmutation takes place without your effort, as a gift of healing.

The healing is instant and natural
as if mental mutation had never happened.
"Oh my goodness, is that what that means?"
Now sit and contemplate and imagine
all of these ego belief burdens falling on the floor,

then you get up and shake yourself like a dog coming in from the rain and it is enough.

Holiness Arising in Holy Transmutation clears the mind of the fog of ego misperception.

Imagine, Holy Love flowing, the Transmuting of the ego mind occurs and mind is healed and then the end with mental silence, as Holy Karma arises once again in Joy and Peace of mind beyond Human understanding.

New Holy Karma thoughts arising, in new forms. A new Holy Form has arisen.

A new willingness: "Here I am. Send me!" "What would you have me do this day?"

I feel that they need a hug.

I can shower some Holy Gold or Holy Love in that direction, to assist in changing their mental state; that is, not letting my right hand know what my left hand is doing or vice versa.

A Holy Agent tethered to Holy Spirit.

You received free, give freely.

Holiness Arising, the meek now inheriting this earth.

The Holy Meek living in singularity with Holy Karma flowing effortlessly.

A New Heaven and a New Earth.

Love to all the Holy Deciders as the Meek living in Holy Karma.

Love to you all from Shamaré

The Protector
The Door Keeper
The Gatekeeper
The Guardian of the Holy Karma Arising Now

18.
Holy Karma > Holiness Lifts Great Burdens

This is one of the most amazing chapters in the book. Enjoy your uplifting!

The Flow of Holy Spirit through any entity now living inside Holy Karma (the Holy Cause and Holy Effect) will progressively have lifted from their Holy Mind what seems like many great ego self-created burdens.

The Entity does not do this lifting itself. It is the Return to True Holy Nature that does the seeming lifting.

Holy Spirit in action.

> Inside the ego misidentification of True Holy Self,
> there are many conforming burdens
> invoked by an ego self.
> This conformity arises in many forms,
> family energy, culture, religion, body and mind health,
> law, music, food, politics, arts, scholarship
> and many more.
>
> Often this mental conformity

> (and often physical conformity
> and even dress conformity),
> is a set of unwritten rules
> that are propagandised as a child grows,
> to become part of a mental ego framework,
> and another earth world human viewpoint
> develops in that one,
>
> in other words, a culture
> (part of an old cult, a grouping idea)
> You are not part of a group; you are Universal.

We could look at all these various ego-designed conformities in detail. However, it is not required.

These types of life complexities will melt away with the arising once again of Holy Singularity and Simplicity in a Holy Mind. They become valueless now!

At the arising of Holy Karma, with the driving force of Holy Self Love, and Holy Self Desire, the cultural conformities may flow away as useless and of no benefit for a Holy Mind. Why bother having them?

> However, some conformities are very sticky
> and they may take some mental attention
> (Surrendering into the forgiveness of Self)
> to get free from them or to allow the process
> of self-dissolving away to take place.
> The undoing of creations,
> the release of value and energy.

This can sometimes be a tricky process, as you unravel. Will it ever end, often is the thought!

Start considering today: do I have ego world conformities? There will be many.

They will show themselves as you loosen up mentally and become more self-aware.

There are no compulsions on releasing ego conformities, it is a personal decision and always be gentle on Holy Self. It will become obvious to drop them, if you desire to move ahead to Holiness.

At some point, this desire to be truly mentally free will override these conformities stickiness and then that new day is upon you. A Holy You starts arising, conformity free (outside of the conforming ego cult).

One of the many conformities that seems pervasive and worldwide in most communities are the strong religious or ideological belief hooks that can weaken or confuse Holy Mental Intentions.

One of these ego mental hooks is the absolute requirement for

a saviour, a guru, a decider, to set you free.

Arising Holy Karma and Holy Awareness no longer require these types of ego saviour hooks.

These types of conformities arise from thoughts of victimisation, separation or being lesser than or incapable of being able. Guilty.

In other words, you are not a Holy Child of God itself but a victim of the ego world, unable to change or heal.

"Once your Holy Freedom Awareness and Holy Desire clicks into place, you will know you have never been a victim of any sort, a rejected one, a faulty one or incapable of having Holy Sovereignty."

You have always been a Holy Child.

Another trick played on many is the conformity to have faith in this or that.

Faith being a supposed educated knowing but with no actual proof, just a strong wishing, they often say with some historical evidence.

On the Arising of Holy Karma in your Holy Mind, faith becomes an obsolete idea.

Divine Knowledge does arise in the Mind of Holy Self and shows your place inside the ALL.

Another cult burden is mentally hoping for salvation of some sort, and this will also be put to rest.

As what is there to hope for,

when you are already Loved
beyond measure, supported
and you received all Holiness,

At your Holy Birth!

Another burden of ego living is the requirement to live in pseudo love, as an ego projection.

This will at last be seen to be erroneous and can be dropped, as True Divine Love flows endlessly in all things, including your Holy Self, effortlessly.

Another great burden,
the actual dominant energy of the ego human mind
and world systems that being self-loathing,
will finally falter and be replaced with Holy Self Love.
Beyond any human understanding possible.

(Ego understanding).

Self-loathing arises when separation from Holy Love Source is believed and that you believe you are powerless to recover it and save yourself.

So, someone else better than you
must save you (a saviour)

and you hate yourself for your weakness.

Another of the many conformities that seems pervasive and worldwide in most communities are the strong nationalistic belief hooks that will weaken or confuse Holy Mental Intentions.

*Know this thoroughly, you are not
a subject of this nation or that,
you are Holy Child. Belonging to a nation or a race
is a mental trap that limits growth or change.*

*See any form of comparison of other nations or race
as worthless and very limiting.*

As these burdens flow away into nothingness and they will, as only creations can, you ascend and transmute back all things to "Holy Love only being Real". The grand realisation! The great lesson learned!

And with this Arising Holy You, a new name arises for you also: "Emmanuel", "God is with us".

Thoughts of ego separation are a thing of the past, that is, not emoted any longer, just something to smile at.

Yes, you are "Divine by Birth and are True Divine Nature", in the Image of, truly, a Holy Child of God.

*A Holy Child of God has no burdens,
only Holy Love flowing endlessly,
not from a source apart from them
but from the one Holy source in the very depth of them.*

This lifting of burdens will happen and naturally,

*do not pressure yourself into change,
allow it to all fall away.*

Holiness has always been there for you, awaiting your embrace.

Love to all the Burden Droppers.

Love to you all from Shamaré

The Protector
The Door Keeper
The Gatekeeper
The Guardian of the Holy Karma Arising Now

19.
Holy Karma > Holiness Relaxes and Expands Awareness and Ability

What will arise as the new framework as Holy Karma takes effect in your life?

Holy Karma
or the Mental state of Holiness,
is naturally relaxed
and in that relaxed environment
awareness and mental ability will expand freely.

This has to be true if you arise from the

Single Point of Consciousness, known as Divinity.

Moving into expanded awareness of Holy Self will lift any and all anxiety.

Moving into expanded awareness and again knowing Holy Family will naturally lift anxiety.

Moving into expanded awareness and allowing Holy Spirit to motivate the action of Holy Karma will release all anxiety. Realising more and more each day.

If anxiety starts arising at any moment, this is an opportunity to step into Holiness further and allow the flow of Holy Karma via the Holy Spirit to ease you into the cause of anxiety. This results in more awareness for expansion of your own Holiness. Step into all arising anxiety moments.

This allowing of Holy Karma to flow,

is simple and natural and desired always.

It will prompt you to just fall into naturally and "Allow, Trust and Embrace" the anxiety feelings that arise in the mind.

This fall into any anxiety feelings

allows the transmutation of the ego fear.

Body-centric ego misidentification reactivities as mental "sprags, or duality leftovers" may jump out every now and then.

This is a splendid opportunity always.

It is just ego projecting and saying try some of this reactivity on for size.

The answer is simple. "Consider it all Joy when" (James).

Start expressing the desire for "Your Akashic

Records" to open to all memory points that trigger anxiety.

The Akashic records will indeed open for you at the correct anxiety items for you. You did store them there.

You will then need to free fall into these anxiety feelings fearlessly.

They are just your seemingly forgotten creations.

You will be able to witness these creations of the past as video, audio, smell and other sensors.

Some will be very old, maybe even right at the point of stepping into the original experience.
"Of what would it be like to live in a domain where "Only Love is Not Real".

Expand into these realisations and the re-membered revelations that flash up for you. Yes, the reveal.

These stored reactive information creations have always been sitting there in your piece of the Akashic database since you first dropped them in as a fearful ego cause event.

If reactivity from original cause events or similar arise again at any point,
this stored ego cause will immediately start
and project out the original effect as mental activity.

*This reactivity jumps up and does its original dance,
producing a fearful memory of mind, like the original".*

*Whenever you call on it,
there is the stored memory
ready to dance for you in your mind,*

as a projection of this ego creation/cause.

Well, why not? You made it all and you asked for it to do this when you hid it away as cause, in fear and denial.

With your newfound Power of Self Love, you can smile as these old reactive records appear, knowing you created them. Amazing.

They will dissolve away because you are choosing now to close the loop on that ego fear anxiety creation and release them as unnecessary, now in your Holiness State.

*Creators running in a misidentified ego mind format
often make creations in states of
fear, guilt and judgement,
then disown the creations
and then move forward in a forgetful manner.*

Disowning the creation, it can be called.

Later on, in an ego reaction, you awaken to them, rediscover them and in Holy Power expand back into the creation time period and say, "Well, blow me down, I did make this thing and I forgot about it."

And it ends that ego creation, as all creations end, when value and purpose is realised, embracing and allowing it to dissolve, in Holy Love Flowing once again. Holy Love does the dissolve.

In many cases, these reactivity causes will dissolve without thought or action, if you allow the Holy Spirit to take them over. You are part of the Holy Spirit and you can pass this work to it.

Holy Spirit is the right-minded part of the All that never entered into the experience of Dualities and has remained Holy always.

You may experience this phenomenon
when the Holy Spirit dissolves the creation
so absolutely that you cannot remember or recall
what reactivity cause you were working on all that time.
You will try to bring to mind what it was,
but it will be thoroughly gone
and not available to you any further.

Not a trace will arise in your mind.

Whatever way the dissolve happens, a pat on the back, six gold stars on the refrigerator door, for your new expansion into Holy Awareness.

Immediately after these dis-creations, new Holy

Abilities will arise on cue; well, not really, they have always been there but unavailable and unknown, due to the mask thrown up by those hidden ego creations with limiting reactivity and thoughts.

You will now find that you will breathe and expand into more Holy Revelation, not just for self but for Holy Self, the Holy One.

You will feel more of the All.

"Ah yes! My friend over there is feeling down today and needs some encouragement."

Day to day, keep opening the records and marvel at your old creations.

You have left quite a trail of stuff, as we all have.

In fact, everything you have ever thought and done is in the records.

Love to all those moving into Holiness, relaxing, expanding awareness with Holy Ability.

Love to you all from Shamaré

The Protector
The Door Keeper
The Gatekeeper
The Guardian of the Holy Karma Arising Now

20.
Holy Karma > Holiness in Heaven on Earth

*Heaven on Earth
will ascend progressively at some point.*

*Whenever you have a Holy Thought,
a Holy Moment in Holy Karma,
the One Mind throughout the Universe reverberates
with the energy of that moment.*

This happens all the time and often with those closest to you, the ones you love while incarnated, and often your body DNA family are aware of the moment in some way.

Sometimes you will connect with one of them often and easily. You will know their emotional state by pausing and feeling them.

When there are enough incarnated Minds in Singularity on earth, that is, running inside Holy Karma again, this effect will become very difficult to ignore and many minds will be affected and changed in a blink.

The arising of Heaven on Earth will follow this course.

*People will start becoming aware without effort,
it will just arise for them. They are ready!*

*The Holy Spirit directing this activity will make sure
that the participants will only be those
who truly desire the change.*

Desire the change now. Get a head start.

Heaven arises in their minds, as the Holy Spirit in conjunction with this desire helps clear out age-old ego patterns and conformities to allow mental freedom again.

The Holy Spirit does not replace these removed patterns and conformities with new ideas or thoughts.

Naturally what arises in these minds is the Birthed Traits of Holy Divinity once again.

No Learning, only allowing of Holy Spirit to work with them and slowly reintegrate them back into Holy Family once again.

Incarnation remains in place.

*Heaven on Earth magically appears
without effort or struggle.
The grand awakening inside incarnation.
The miracle being created
by Holy Awakening Holy Minds.*

*The release of the game of Dualities,
with Love Flowing silently to all
without distortion or modification.*

*How else could it possibly be?
Imagine this happening!*

*No engineered or manipulated outcomes.
Now as it real is!*

Just simplicity once again.

There will be no reversals on this process. It will be unstoppable.

Some who are so conformed or in deep denial of Holy Self will be moved to a new Domain to continue the process of disentanglement. This is because the "Holy All" does not judge them as failed, just taking their time to move back to Holiness.

The final point will come at some moment when all the "Lost Holy Children" will find the bread crumbs trail home to great celebration.

However, Heaven on Earth has precedent at this time and will flow out.

A musing of the old duality game may happen but most likely the lessons will have been thoroughly integrated into consciousness that it will be part of the "New Holy Natural".

Love to you all from Shamaré

The Protector
The Door Keeper
The Gatekeeper
The Guardian of the Holy Karma Arising Now

21.
Holy Karma > Holiness in All Things

Holiness can only ever be truly seen and understood by a Mind that is running in Holy Karma.

*However, sometimes Holiness
can be glimpsed and remembered,
even by an incarnated soul running an ego mind
because Holiness can shine through*

and stir old memories of ancient times and Holy Family.

Many will start their journey based on this simple but powerful happening when meeting a Holy One.

And because Holiness is based in Reality, it is therefore colour blind to ego projection and sees no judgement.

One in ego projection can also still hear Holiness Words and these words may stir them deep down.

*As ego projection is just created foolishness
or a form of created insanity
in the eyes of one running in Holy Karma,
it means nothing to the Holy one.*

*There is therefore no judgement on anything,
as it is not real to be judged or assessed.*

*Hence it is a muse more than anything else
to the Holy One.
(How is this possible?)*

Holy Eyes in Simplicity and Singularity

only ever see Holy Love Flowing.

When a Holy One allows Holy Love as it is in Singularity, all is as it is meant to be.

A Holy Mind in Holy Karma acknowledges this and does not spend any time on it, it is as it is.

This is the Natural in Holiness or as it is in Holiness always.

*A Mind in Holy Karma
that assess ego projection and misperception,
see it as nothing,
only an aberration of mind
that is based in non-realities.*

*Of no value but harmless
as it is just an aberrant creation. Not real!*

So, no thought can be given to this as this is the desire, decision and outcome of the ego mind involved whether they are aware of it or not.

So, there you have it in simplicity.

*Holiness in All Things is a rare truth,
not understood by many yet.*

Not lived by many yet!

At a future time even inside incarnated creations, it will be the natural state for all in the new heaven and new earth, the Holy new society of humans.

It cannot be any other way for love to flow freely.

You will know when you are this state, as it will be as if a switch has been turned on in the mind.

Love to all the eyes that see

"Only Holiness in All Things".

The end of the original question, as we have all experienced living in a creation where "Only Love is not Real" and then awakened fully, realising we prefer "Only Love is Real".

It was innocent, no one was hurt, all will recover Joy and Peace of Mind back in the loving (metaphorical) arms of Holy Family once again.

Love to all those moving to "Only Seeing Holiness now", having transition to Holy Karma once again.

Love to you all from Shamaré

The Protector
The Door Keeper
The Gatekeeper
The Guardian of the Holy Karma Arising Now

22.
Holy Karma > Holiness as Divine Wholeness

As we draw to a close in the book, Holiness is re-established, the grand purpose of the book, Holy Karma flowing effortlessly once again.

Our last chapter together in Holy Contemplation using the One Holy Mind as the sketch pad. Yes, this is where we have been working, talking, imagining and planning, right inside Divinity itself. That is how close it all is to you, less than the width of a thought!

Please hold all this Holy Information as dear (Worthship) to your heart and in your Holy Mind at all times. Lock it in with strong desire, intention, allowance and surrender.

(The heart is the metaphorical seat of divine motivation.)

In other words, hold it as great value, your treasure.

Bathe your Holy Mind daily in contemplation of your Holiness, manifesting this via Holy Karma in Surrender.

All the Holy Children,
even the ones in the depths of the world system
with massive humanity ego misidentification
and deep insanity,

are Holy and remain so forever.

See this clearly! See with the "Eyes of the Christ Mind", only and always.

Do not be beguiled by ego any further, to judge what you imagine is there. Smile lovingly at it.

This Holiness is even true when perceiving insane beliefs and actions that may indicate otherwise.

An unaware soul
who is not yet accessing Holy Knowledge,
and running mentally
inside the envelope of Holy Karma,
will judge this behaviour
as proof of the others' unholiness.

There is no condemnation or judgement
inside Holy Karma or Holiness.
How could Holiness judge Holiness?

Do not Judge, lest you be judged.
(By ego self of course
and projecting the judgement out at peers).

Holiness is singularity,
without the duality of ego Judgement.

*There is only Holy Love Flowing,
inside Holy Truth*

and Holy Reality with Holy Karma.

If you are still vacillating on this, consider.

The insanity exhibited by the unaware is not real.

It is a creation of a mind in misunderstanding and misperception of Holy Self; that is all, an aberration that can be healed.

That mind has substituted an ego self into the Holy Child equation of life, in error.

It is only a projection from an ego mind, as a dream creation, a dysfunctional mind, thoroughly insane.

Therefore, because it is a creation and sustained by the dreamer, it is not permanent (unless chosen).

Holiness remains as the unchangeable base state always, for All the Holy Children.

Do not forget, we are Multi-Dimensional Entities, spanning many dimensions, with much/most of our consciousness remaining inside Holiness at all times.

*Holiness is everywhere you look,
even if using incarnated eyes
and it is everywhere else you can imagine*

where consciousness dwells.

And do imagine.

Holiness is You (Yourself always Holy).

Holiness is vast when put beside the small earth, the world and humanity ego misidentification shadow.

Earth, the world and humanity as ego misidentification resides inside the Holy Mind as a dream for a few.

All Arise from Holiness, in perfection, as a mirror image of the original model, the Divine, God Itself.

Inside Holy Karma, the reflection always seen is "Holy and Complete".

Allow Holy Karma, directed by the Holy Spirit, to envelop you at all moments to see Holiness in Clarity.

You are Loved always and are Holy always.

And with that short ending, I will withdraw once again to allow deep contemplation and healing to occur in your Holy Mind, as Children of the Holiness itself.

This may be truly emotional for you all as you read

on to the conclusion.
Allow it to flow.

Blessed are all those moving into Holiness in Decision, for they walk with God.

Blessed are all those moving into Holiness Arising, for they become a bright beacon of Holy Light.

Blessed are all those moving into Holiness in Self Love, for they show **"Only Love is Real".**

Blessed are all those moving into Holiness in Clarity, for they will certainly shape many dimensions.

Blessed are all those moving into Holiness in Joy, for they will heal many minds without a word.

Blessed are all those moving into Holiness in Peace of Mind, for they can sit alone and change the world.

Blessed are all those moving into Holiness in Communication, for they will talk to millions, seen and unseen.

Blessed are all those moving into Holiness in Being, for they will transform many things effortlessly.

Blessed are all those moving into Holiness in

Actions, for they are feeding Holy Love to all minds.

Blessed are all those moving into Holiness in Serving, for they will divide and serve more than fish and loaves.

Blessed are all those moving into Holiness in Transparency, for they will become Angelic in the process.

Blessed are all those moving into Holiness in Transformation, for they have found God in themselves.

Blessed are all those moving into Holiness in Transmutation, for they will radiate and show **"Only Love is Real"**.

Blessed are all those moving into Holiness in Lifting a Great Burden, for they will sing songs of praise.

Blessed are all those moving into Holiness in Relaxing and Expanding Awareness and Ability, for they will be the peacemakers and the Holy Manifesters.

Blessed are all those moving into Holiness bringing Heaven to Earth, for they will become the new inhabitants of the new Holy Way of Life, even inside a creation.

Blessed are all those seeing Holiness in All Things, for they walk as Christ once again.

Blessed are all those moving into Divine Wholeness, for they are gods themselves.

Love to you all from Shamaré until the next time

The Protector
The Door Keeper
The Gatekeeper
The Guardian of the Holy Karma Arising Now

Addendum 1

Holiness Review

**For you, who are now aware
and accept your own Holiness.**

I Am Holy

I now dwell in the flow of Holy Karma once again.

I have returned to Holy Singularity.

I have Awakened from the ego dream of Divine Separation.

I have chosen to be Only Holy once again.

I cherish and feel the flow of Holy Divine Love.

I am aware of my deep connection to Holy Consciousness, as the one thing that really exists.

The Holy Love that flows in me is from the very depth of Holy Me, from Holy Source.

The grand virtual experience of living in ego duality and awakening inside this is now complete.

I have brought Heaven to Earth for myself and flow it out via Holy Karma in Holy Mental Surrender.

Once again, a Christ walks the Earth.

Many will call this one Emmanuel; God is with us (again).

I flow out Holy Love through Holy Karma, as the Holy Spirit in action.

All is made anew in Holiness.

And so, it is so. Amen.

Love to you all from Shamaré

The Protector
The Door Keeper
The Gatekeeper
The Guardian of the Holy Karma Arising Now

Addendum 2

Holy Karma > Preparing your Holy Mind for the Holy Trek of no Distance, to a Place you have never left

You will be tried many times and may even feel incapable of continuing this Holy Journey.

It can be very challenging. Everything you have created to stop the process will come up for you.

But know this that Holy Family is unlimited Joy and Peace beyond human understanding.

There are only two thought systems that only really exist; you have to choose which one is for you.

The first, the Holy thought system, is based on "I am but Spirit, everything else is illusion. I dwell in Holy Love flowing in singularity and simplicity where '**Only Love is Real**'".

The second thought system is based on "I am but body DNA, an intelligent animal full of misperception and living in struggle, dualities and complexity. Hades on earth."

So here are some thoughts to help restore you when moments of doubt arise for you, as they will.

1. How close are you to Holiness and Divinity at any moment? Realise and know this.
2. Your Consciousness arises from a single point of Holy Intelligence. You are alive and know this gift. It is you.
3. Your Awareness arises inside Holy Consciousness, it can't come from any other source. Are you now aware of this?
4. Your day-to-day mental activity accesses Divinity every moment via the gift of the One Holy Mind. Your thoughts moment by moment flow inside this one Holy Mind.
5. You are not the DNA; You drive the robot remotely always. You are not just Jim or Mary! Know this thoroughly.
6. You are therefore closer to divinity than the width of a thought. You are intimately connected at all moments without ceasing, to Divinity. Nothing else is possible. You would not exist.
7. This is not beliefs; this is a moment-by-moment experience. Feel this and appreciate divinity.
8. If you think you have failed in some way it doesn't change the intimacy of your connection. The failure is only a thought to be

released when you allow Holy Self Love, Holy Karma to flow once again.
9. Holy Love flows to you and through you continually without ceasing, not from a source apart from you but from the source in the very depth of you. You are the well of Divine Love!
10. This indicates that as a Holy Child you can only ever be one with Divinity, there is no gap, it is all illusion. Even when you have mad thoughts, your connection stays with the Divine one mind.
11. Do love the singularity energy of the grand Holy Intelligence flowing endlessly and without cost as a forever gift to you as your birth right as one of the Holy Children.
12. Take your birth right gift and wallow in it until you once again feel as the Pure Spirit you are, just having experience in a duality created world that you have volunteered to mentally project into for experience.

That is enough to rebuild your Divine Trust once again.

Your Trust will be tested many times. Come back again for a refresher.

Sit and reflect to regain energy once again.

Read the next Addendum.

Love to you all from Shamaré

The Protector
The Door Keeper
The Gatekeeper
The Guardian of the Holy Karma Arising Now

Addendum 3

Holy Karma > I release the need… A Universal Statement to Start the Healing of your Holy Mind!

*The Need in each of these statements
and any statement you develop,
is highlighting that there is something in the way,
a cause, that is in the way of the healing.
This Need is held in place
and believed to be of benefit to you, some value.
Identify the Need and this will lead you to the cause
that you have placed in your Holy Mind to divert you
from Holiness.*

The value in the Need can be released once you know you are not stuck anymore and you have the power to release and heal yourself. Choose again!

I release the need to feel inadequate.

I release the need to feel being stuck.

I release the need to think I am right.

I release the need to struggle.

I release the need to feel unloved.

I release the need to find the correct words.

I release the need to feel being a victim.

I release the need to be intellectual.

I release the need to be political.

I release the need to be religious.

You have a turn also. Make them fit well with your emotions.

I release the need to be —————-?! Fill in the blank.

To find your words to fill in the blank, fall into the feeling you are having, sit in the feeling until the words come up for you. You will know, as your mind will still once you recognise and say the words.

If you need to sit with a close friend that loves you and they may read your mind for you and tell you the words out of love for you. This is very common. They also may know what you are resisting and in compassion link up with you. Two passions together are better than one sometimes. Compassion.

Love to all the Holy Children in incarnation now.

Choose to move to Holy Karma flow,
bringing Heaven to Earth
as a result of that powerful choice.

Enjoy and Love the hell out of the struggle.

Love to you all from Shamaré

The Protector
The Door Keeper
The Gatekeeper
The Guardian of the Holy Karma Arising Now

Addendum 4

Availability of the Information to your Holy Mind

You may well swear you have read this book cover to cover; however, what takes root in the mind is always only a subsection of the entirety.

If you put this book away for some time and come back for a second read after you have mentally moved on, you may well swear you have never read some sections.

This process will continue as the actual meaning of the words get deeper and deeper in your mind.

This is not to be taken that there is something wrong with you, it just goes back to the first two sentences that started this appendix.

This happening is really a form of encouragement, as each read exposes how you have changed in some way and how your Holy Mind is opening for a deeper appreciation.

If you find you have preconceived ideas about Holiness and it precludes you, you may need to allow time for the changes to take place.

You will know you are free when you can say out loud to another person, "I am Holiness itself, a Loved Begotten Child of God".

This will be an indicator for you and now you can read the book fully from then on or not.

Much the same as saying "I and my Father are one!"

This will indeed be a great encouragement on that day.

Sitting and reflecting with some inner voice prompting is often required to move into a deeper space.

This deeper space is very deep, and this process will continue for a long period of time, with your appreciation going up and down, until it is locked solid.

Each day see yourself sitting in the Christ Mind and see no gap but only Holy Family.

This day will come. Your Holiness will reveal itself. Self-Love will win the day. Holy Karma will arise.

Love to you all from Shamaré

The Protector
The Door Keeper
The Gatekeeper
The Guardian of the Holy Karma Arising Now

About the Author

Shamaré lives in remote hills in Northland, New Zealand, surrounded by forests, birds, animals, streams and nature. From an early age, he knew that the world he was being shown was missing some essential knowledge. This knowledge, as spiritual writings from Shamaré, has been shared worldwide to a private group of friends for more than 20 years.

His commission now is to bring this knowledge to mainstream readers worldwide, to share a vision of the future where humanity can finally bring heaven to earth as a reality. Shamaré (designated as the Guardian, Door Keeper, Gate Keeper and Protector) is now a public instructor of this knowledge and is available to meet your group of friends to share and expand this knowledge.

Shamaré's teachings may very well become the opening and support you need in your own pathway to awakening fully.

www.shamare.com

Other Books by the Author

Spirituality 101–601 and Beyond

This book unlocks these possibilities in any person by awakening their own Spirituality, just by following simple mind lessons. The unlocking occurs as you learn to let love flow to you and through you, not from a source apart from you, but the source of love deep inside yourself.

www.ingramcontent.com/pod-product-compliance
Lightning Source LLC
Chambersburg PA
CBHW062032290426
44109CB00026B/2600